# THE
# 50 FINAL
# EVENTS
## IN WORLD
## HISTORY

# Also by Robert J. Morgan

*Always Near*
*Beyond Reasonable Doubt*
*Every Child Every Nation Every Day*
*God Works All Things Together for Your Good*
*Great Is Thy Faithfulness*
*Mastering Life Before It's Too Late*
*Reclaiming the Lost Art of Biblical Meditation*
*The Jordan River Rules*
*The Red Sea Rules*
*The Strength You Need*
*Then Sings My Soul*
*Worry Less, Live More*

# THE 50 FINAL EVENTS IN WORLD HISTORY

## THE BIBLE'S LAST WORDS ON EARTH'S FINAL DAYS

ROBERT J. MORGAN

W PUBLISHING GROUP

AN IMPRINT OF THOMAS NELSON

*To John Campbell*

# Contents

# The Trajectory of Our Times

Every day the sun rises and sets, etching another sentence of history onto the parchment of our times. The tiny blue marble of earth, suspended in the vastness of a spangled universe, spins on its axis while its inhabitants cling for life. People are fearful. Our world is in disarray, and who knows what will happen to us and to our children? Who knows what tomorrow holds?

Almighty God knows.

He knows what's ahead. He knows it perfectly, instantly, totally, and omnisciently. He knows the future as well as the past, and the outlines of His predetermined plans are engraved on the pages of His Book. The Intelligent Creator is an Infallible Communicator, and He has packed His Word with remarkable predictions, like a woman packing remnants into her quilting chest.

I'm convinced a phenomenal pattern is about to unfold. World events aren't lurching into chaos; they are moving toward culmination and consummation. There's hope for tomorrow, and there's hope for you and yours. The cascading flow of crises is merging with the outlines of Bible prophecy, like two mighty rivers crashing into each other and coalescing into an unstoppable flood. For the children of God, this isn't a flood that will sweep us away. It will lift us up!

We need this kind of uplifting hope. Everyone I know seems

to have a lot of unexpected stress. Looming over the demanding details of daily life are gathering clouds of worldwide cataclysm. We are living in perilous times. The world has always been in a mess, but not since the days of Noah has our fragile planet faced such imminent and existential dangers as now. The threats—nuclear, economic, technological, philosophical, moral, political, biological, viral, environmental, and a host of others—imperil the earth with calamities of biblical proportions, which is what this book is about.

In these last days, when breaking news hits us at the speed of light, it's vital to understand scriptural prophecy and to have a firm grasp on the Bible's last words about earth's final days. As no prior generation, we need to understand the contents of the book of Revelation, which opens with these words: *The revelation from Jesus Christ, which God gave him to show his servants what must soon take place* (1:1).

## Me?

Perhaps you're thinking, *Me? Study Revelation?*

Absolutely! Nothing is more exciting than knowing tomorrow in advance, especially when tomorrow is hurtling toward us with unprecedented trouble. How exhilarating to stand on the precipice of prophecy, peering through the mist into the mysterious days predicted in the Bible's final book! History moves in only one direction—never backward, always onward, toward its final preappointed end. It grinds relentlessly into tomorrow, oblivious to the catastrophes and cataclysms in its wake.

Dr. J. Barton Payne, a Bible scholar and seminary professor who served on the translation committees for the *New American Standard Bible* and the *New International Version*, analyzed the prophetic portions of Scripture and calculated that of the roughly 31,000 verses in the Bible, over 8,000 contain predictive prophecy—8,352 verses to be exact. In other words, about 27 percent of the Bible is prophetic. Some of those prophecies were historical or messianic predictions, which have already been fulfilled, but many still point toward the future—including much of the material in the final book of the Bible, Revelation.[1]

Since prophecy is a subject that interests God and occupies His Word, it should intrigue our minds and thrill our hearts, especially in these tense days. All the other books of the Bible lead to Revelation. It's how God chose to conclude Holy Scripture. The preceding sixty-five books pave the way for the twenty-two chapters that compose the Revelation of Saint John, the sixty-sixth and final book of the Bible.

Without Revelation, the Bible would have no satisfying conclusion. It would end with the book of Jude, which is a wonderful epistle about contending for the faith but is not a book that heralds God's plans for time and eternity.

Revelation is the terminal toward which the train of history is traveling, and we're all aboard for the ride. The events it describes are forthcoming. That's why I'm keen to study Revelation and to teach its truths to others. It gives me affirmation, answers, assurance, anticipation, and a call to action, enabling me to stand stronger for Christ in my generation.

I'm deeply troubled when I think that perhaps 80 or 90 percent of Christians, in my estimation—even those who have been attending church for years—are baffled by Revelation. It's understandable in a way, because Revelation is full of apocalyptic images. But this isn't a sustainable condition for any growing Christian. As never before, we need God's answers about our future!

My goal is to demystify the book of Revelation for you. I've examined this remarkable book for fifty years and taught through it many times. I've concluded that the simplest way to understand Revelation is to take it as literally as possible and as sequentially as possible. Using that approach, I think I can help anyone understand its content.

The last book of the Bible is not named *Obscurity* or *Puzzlement* or *Ambiguity*. It's called *Revelation*, for God wants to *reveal* His future to His children. This is the ultimate consummation for which all the Bible was given and toward which all history is moving. It is the glorious hope for which every child of God is waiting.

It's time you understood this book from its first phrase to its last verse.

It's time to know the fifty final events in world history. I cannot tell you when these events will begin unfolding. It may be before you finish reading this book, or it could be ten years from now—or a hundred years or more. Jesus said, "It is not for you to know the times or dates the Father has set by his own authority" (Acts 1:7). But it *is* for us to study His Word, including its fabulous final installment—Revelation.

## Him!

To stay healthy of heart, we need anticipation, expectation, something to look forward to. Anticipation is the secret of hope, and hope is the key to mental health. Whether it's finishing a medical treatment, taking a long-planned trip, awaiting the birth of a baby, planning for graduation, or nearing a milestone, we need a future event to keep us going. With Christ, it's not just a future event we're awaiting; it's a coming King. Today more than ever we need *Someone* to look forward to.

In Revelation, we meet Jesus as we've never seen Him before—as a King enthroned in glory, walking among golden lampstands, presiding over the epochs of time and eternity, and shining like the sun in its brilliance. He is receiving the praises of ten thousand times ten thousand, returning to earth as a conquering hero, and reigning forever as the Lion, the Lamb, and the Lord of all. The book of Revelation puts the finishing touches on the biblical portrait of Jesus, letting us see Him as He is in His eternal state, as the Root and Offspring of David, the Bright and Morning Star, the King of kings and Lord of lords, and the illuminating force of New Jerusalem.

Our conception of Jesus is incomplete without the descriptions of Him in Revelation, and as you study these twenty-two chapters, you'll see Him with new appreciation and love Him with heightened recognition for all the glories of His person and His position of supreme authority.

That's why I love the book of Revelation. It's about Jesus, and it's about tomorrow, which is right on schedule. It cannot be rushed or delayed, and it will arrive on time whether we're ready or not. For those who know and understand the final book of the Bible, the future is worth thinking about. The events of Revelation are well worth studying. In fact, great blessings come into our lives when we devote our attention to the incredible 404 verses that make up Revelation. This is the only book in the Bible that begins and ends by pronouncing special blessings on those who study, understand, obey, and share its truth.

> *Our conception of Jesus is incomplete without the descriptions of Him in Revelation.*

> *Blessed is the one who reads aloud the words of this prophecy, and blessed are those who hear it and take to heart what is written in it, because the time is near.* (1:3)

> *Look, I am coming soon! Blessed is the one who keeps the words of the prophecy written in this scroll.* (22:7)

Let's claim these blessings as we move through the pages of Revelation and discover God's prophetic road map for the coming days of adventure and apocalypse, which will soon engulf our world and usher in the endless ages of eternity.

# How to Get the Most out of This Book

The goal of this book is to demystify the book of Revelation, helping you grasp and apply its contents. Let me suggest getting a good copy of a modern translation of the Bible and a sharp pencil or a pen that won't bleed through the pages, and doing the following:

1. Draw dividing lines between the following chapters (see example, opposite page):
   - Chapters 1 and 2—This delineates chapter 1 as the prologue of the book, and you can write the word *Prologue* over chapter 1. Over chapter 2, write the words *Messages to the Seven Churches.*
   - Chapters 3 and 4—Over chapter 4, write *Worship in Heaven.*
   - Chapters 5 and 6—Over chapter 6, write *First Half of Tribulation.*
   - Chapters 11 and 12—Over chapter 12, write *Middle of Tribulation.*
   - Chapters 13 and 14—Over chapter 14, write *Last Half of Tribulation.*
   - Chapters 18 and 19—Over chapter 19, write *Return of Christ and Thousand-Year Reign.*
   - Chapters 20 and 21—Over chapter 21, write *Our Eternal Home.*
   - These mark the major divisions of Revelation. Keep your open Bible beside you as you read *The 50 Final Events in World History.*
2. As you work your way through the fifty final events, number each one in the margin of your Bible (see example, opposite page). This will help you follow the book's unfolding content.

3. As you read, ask God for insight into the meaning and application of the book of Revelation. A good prayer is "Open my eyes that I may see wonderful things in your law" (Psalm 119:18).

---

mouth. [17]You say, 'I am rich; I have acquired wealth and do not need a thing.' But you do not realize that you are wretched, pitiful, poor, blind and naked. [18]I counsel you to buy from me gold refined in the fire, so you can become rich; and white clothes to wear, so you can cover your shameful nakedness; and salve to put on your eyes, so you can see.

[19]Those whom I love I rebuke and discipline. So be earnest and repent. [20]Here I am! I stand at the door and knock. If anyone hears my voice and opens the door, I will come in and eat with that person, and they with me.

[21]To the one who is victorious, I will give the right to sit with me on my throne, just as I was victorious and sat down with my Father on his throne. [22]Whoever has ears, let them hear what the Spirit says to the churches."

*Worship in Heaven*

**The Throne in Heaven**

(1) **4** After this I looked, and there before me was a door standing open in heaven. And the voice I had first heard speaking to me like a trumpet said, "Come up here, and I will show you what must take place after this." (2) [2]At once I was in the Spirit, and there before me was a throne in heaven with someone sitting on it. [3]And the one who sat there had the appearance of jasper and ruby. A rainbow that shone like an emerald encircled the throne. [4]Surrounding the throne were twenty-four other thrones, and seated on them were twenty-four elders. They were dressed in white and had crowns of gold on their heads. [5]From the throne came flashes of lightning, rumblings and peals of thunder. In front of the throne, seven lamps were

blazing. These are the seven spirits[a] of God. [6]Also in front of the throne there was what looked like a sea of glass, clear as crystal.

In the center, around the throne, were four living creatures, and they were covered with eyes, in front and in back. [7]The first living creature was like a lion, the second was like an ox, the third had a face like a man, the fourth was like a flying eagle. [8]Each of the four living creatures had six wings and was covered with eyes all around, even under its wings. Day and night they never stop saying:

" 'Holy, holy, holy
  is the Lord God Almighty,'[b]
  who was, and is, and is to come."

[9]Whenever the living creatures give glory, honor and thanks to him who sits on the throne and who lives for ever and ever, [10]the twenty-four elders fall down before him who sits on the throne and worship him who lives for ever and ever. They lay their crowns before the throne and say:

[11]"You are worthy, our Lord
  and God,
  to receive glory and honor
    and power,
for you created all things,
  and by your will they were
    created
  and have their being."

**The Scroll and the Lamb**

**5** Then I saw in the right hand of him who sat on the throne a scroll with writing on both sides and sealed with seven seals. [2]And I saw a mighty angel proclaiming in a loud voice, "Who is worthy to break the seals and open

---
[a] 5 That is, the sevenfold Spirit
[b] 8 Isaiah 6:3

PART 1

# THE STARTING POINT

*Revelation 1–3*

# CHAPTER 1

# The Hidden Code for Understanding Revelation

A few years ago when I had a rigorous trip to Branson, Missouri, for a speaking engagement, I asked my college intern, Carson, to come with me and help with the driving. In Branson, I spoke several times, then we fastened our seat belts for the drive home. "Since we have seven or eight hours on the road tonight," I said to him, "what do you want to talk about?"

"I want to understand the book of Revelation," Carson said. "Could you walk me through each chapter while I drive?"

Reaching into my backpack, I pulled out my Bible and turned to its final twenty pages. I started with Revelation 1:1, and we worked through each of the twenty-two chapters as we drove through the night. As I thumbed through one chapter after another, reading it aloud, going verse by verse, I saw something I'd never noticed. I was astounded I had never seen a particular pattern so clearly before.

What I discovered I consider to be the key to decoding Revelation—but it isn't original to me. Many expositors have pointed it out before; it's one of the most obvious features of the book. But I had never seen it myself before that long drive with Carson.

The very next day when I left to lead a tour to Israel, I took my Bible with me and pondered the book of Revelation the whole way. Standing on the Mount of Olives with its million-dollar view of Jerusalem, I gathered my group and taught as clearly as I could what the Bible predicts about the future. Throughout the trip, I kept thinking through the contents of Revelation, and my conviction grew stronger that there is a simple arrangement to the book that is often overlooked.

Here, I believe, is the key to decoding the book of Revelation and unlocking its truth: There is an alternating pattern from passage to passage throughout the book of Revelation. The scene shifts from heaven to earth and from earth back to heaven. The action fluctuates between what's happening below and what's happening above. It's as though a spotlight rhythmically pivots up and down, transmitting insights from heaven regarding events down here. In learning to appreciate this pattern, we can learn to interpret not just future events but also present circumstances in light of heaven's wisdom.

## The Undergirding Structure of Revelation

Let me show you in abbreviated fashion how this unfolds throughout Revelation. If you want to open your Bible, you can trace this for yourself using the following bullet points as a guide, or you can scan these points below and easily comprehend the pattern. Don't worry about the content of each passage. We'll deal with that later. For now, just notice how the point of view zigzags back and forth from heaven to earth.

- **On Earth: John on Patmos (Revelation 1:1–11).** The action begins on earth as the book opens with John's description of his exile to the penal island of Patmos. As John was the last surviving member of the original twelve apostles, his presence in the city of Ephesus was problematic to Roman officials, who banished him to this small island in the Aegean.

- **In Heaven: The Glorified Christ (Revelation 1:12–20).** In Revelation 1:12, the scene changes to heaven, where John saw the glorified Christ. *I turned around to see the voice that was speaking to me,* John wrote. *And when I turned I saw . . . someone like a son of man* (Revelation 1:12–13). Suddenly Patmos didn't seem so bad, for it was illumined by heaven.

- **On Earth: The Seven Churches (Revelation 2:1–3:22).** In chapter 2, the scene shifts back to earth and to the condition of the seven churches in John's congregational circuit, which is described in Revelation 2–3.

- **In Heaven: The Throne at the Beginning of the Tribulation (Revelation 4:1–5:14).** Then the action shifts back to heaven and to the future. In chapters 4–5, John witnessed the glorious celebration that will occur as the heavenly hosts hail the beginning of the onset of events leading to the second coming of Christ. These two chapters describe the greatest scene of worship we have in the entire Bible, but they also represent a courtroom scene in which God is preparing to judge evil on the earth.

- **On Earth: The Seven Seals (Revelation 6:1–7:8).** The camera pans back to earth in Revelation 6–7 as the seven seals are opened, giving us the course of events composing the first part of the tribulation period. The outpouring of judgment begins.

- **In Heaven: The Great Multitude (Revelation 7:9–8:5).** Once again we're caught up to heaven to see the great multitude of angels and tribulation martyrs around the throne of God.

- **On Earth: The Seven Trumpets (Revelation 8:6–11:14).** In Revelation 8:6, the focus shifts downward again to show the unfolding events on earth during the blasting of the seven trumpets.

- **In Heaven: Thunderous Praise Around the Throne (Revelation 11:15–19).** In the last half of Revelation 11, the action shifts back to heaven as resounding praise accompanies the events taking place on earth, because *the kingdom of the world has become the kingdom of our Lord and of his Messiah, and he will reign for ever and ever* (v. 15).

- **On Earth: The Anti-Trinity (Revelation 12:1–13:18).** These passages return us to earth as we watch the formation of a diabolical trinity, an evil trio of agents who will unleash a reign of terror that will turn the last half of the tribulation into a period of great tribulation.

- **In Heaven: The Lamb Is Worshiped (Revelation 14:1–5).** Then we're again caught up to heaven to witness the arrival of the 144,000 faithful witnesses who have escaped the carnage of earth.

- **On Earth: Angels of Judgment, Bowls of Wrath, and the Collapse of Babylon (Revelation 14:6–18:24).** The last catastrophic events of the great tribulation unfold in chapters 14–18, as seven angels pour out their bowls of wrath on the earth, climaxing in the battle of Armageddon and in a global earthquake that will obliterate the great cities of the world.

- **In Heaven: The Hallelujah Chorus (Revelation 19:1–16).** As the final cataclysms devastate our planet, the scene shifts back to heaven where a hallelujah chorus bursts forth from every voice of the angelic hosts. Amid their praise Christ will descend to earth, returning as He promised.

- **On Earth: The Return of Christ and Its Aftermath (Revelation 19:17–20:15).** The next passages are focused on earth as Christ returns, takes charge of planet earth, and ushers in a thousand years of peace.

- **In Heaven: Eternity Begins (Revelation 21:1–22:21).** At the end of the book of Revelation, heaven and earth are merged together as one in the new heaven and the new earth. Eternity arrives for the children of God.

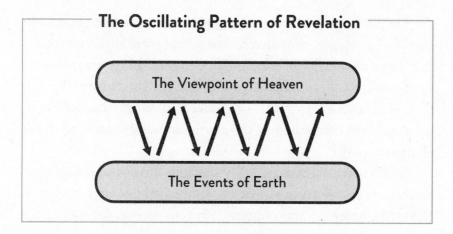

The Oscillating Pattern of Revelation

The Viewpoint of Heaven

The Events of Earth

## The Underlying Lesson for Us

Now that you clearly see this alternating pattern between the action on earth and the response in heaven, I hope you can see I'm not giving you a conspiracy theory, a wild idea, or some strange new way of interpreting the future. This pattern is clearly woven into the structure of the Bible's last book.

When things look darkest on earth, they seem brightest in heaven. As earth churns through its terrible tribulations, heaven erupts in celebration because evil is collapsing and sin and suffering are slipping away.

This isn't just a literary formula for understanding the Bible's most baffling book. It's the scriptural way to decode the baffling events of life. The pattern of looking at earthly events from a heavenly point of view has significance for us beyond the contents of Revelation. The earthly/heavenly perspective can provide a scaffolding for the totality of our thinking about all of life. Everything changes when we view the events here *below* with a perspective from *above*. We begin thinking like Christians, like Christ. Seeing things as they appear from above changes our attitudes about everything every day.

The Bible says, "Our light and momentary troubles are achieving for us an eternal glory that far outweighs them all. So we fix our eyes not on what is seen, but on what is unseen, since what is seen is temporary, but what is unseen is eternal" (2 Corinthians 4:17–18).

The apostle Paul wrote, "I consider that our present sufferings are not worth comparing to the glory that will be revealed in us" (Romans 8:18).

God has said to humans, "My thoughts are not your thoughts, neither are your ways my ways. . . . As the heavens are higher than the earth, so are my ways higher than your ways and my thoughts than your thoughts" (Isaiah 55:8–9).

And James 3:13–18 says there is wisdom from below and wisdom from above. We achieve true wisdom only when we view the events of earth from the perspective of heaven. We must understand, as best we can, our daily affairs from God's vantage point.

Recently I was at the Houston airport when I received word that my first and oldest friend had been diagnosed with cancer. He and I are the same age, and when we were young our dads had adjoining orchards on the Tennessee–North Carolina border. We played among the apple trees and worked together in the packinghouse. Hearing the news, I immediately called him. I was unprepared for what he said. "Yes, and my cancer is rapid and terminal. I've chosen to bypass treatment. I watched my dad go through cancer treatments, and I don't want to go through what he did, especially since my condition is so advanced."

My eyes filled up and I couldn't respond. But David continued, "It's all right, though. I'm sad about leaving my family, but I trusted Jesus as my Savior when I was nine years old. I'm excited to see what's next. I'm ready for heaven."

Shortly afterward, my friend slipped from earth to heaven as he held in his mind the truths and joys and reunions and promises contained in our heaven-sent book. When I spoke by his graveside, I recalled our conversation and spoke of his divine perspective.

Across all the vectors of life, God's Word gives us heaven's commentary on our earthly days, and by reading His sixty-six books—including the last one—we look at life with wisdom from above. We can't deal adequately with world events or personal crises unless we increasingly see things from Christ's perspective on the throne. When we view things horizontally, we feel confusion; but when we see things vertically, life makes sense—including the direction of history. Everything changes when we interpret events below with wisdom from above and see things as the Lord does in heaven.

Every day is different when lived with anticipation. Every situation changes when viewed through the lens of Scripture. Every circumstance is manageable when we see it from the perspective of the eternal throne of our soon-coming Christ. The book of Revelation may appear to be filled with apocalyptic catastrophes, unrivaled since the beginning of the world and never to be equaled again—a world torn apart at the seams. But from the Divine Author's vantage point, it's a celebration of evil defeated, earth redeemed, Christ enthroned, and paradise regained.

And that brings us to the first verse of the first chapter—Revelation 1:1:

*The revelation from Jesus Christ, which God gave him to show his*
*servants what must soon take place.*

# CHAPTER 2

# Next Stop: Patmos
## *Revelation 1*

Over the years, I've had opportunities to travel widely, and I always ask myself if I'd enjoy living in whatever location I'm visiting. Everyone occasionally wonders what it would be like to live elsewhere. Sometimes we watch real estate shows on television and fantasize about buying a home in an exotic locale. *Would I enjoy island life? What about living in the heart of a pulsating city? How about a village in the Alps or along the California coast?*

Where would you live if you could choose any destination on earth?

*Forbes* magazine published an article on Europe's most idyllic locations—places that are tranquil, beautiful, and rich with heritage. Their top suggestion was a small island in the Aegean Sea known as Patmos. With a population of about three thousand on thirteen square miles, Patmos offers peace and quiet. It has no airport; the only way to get there is by ferry. The interior of the island is beautiful, and its beaches are pristine. The temperatures are moderate all year, and most days are sunny. The cost of living is relatively low, and the island bears a rich heritage of religious significance.[1]

Much of that religious significance is bound up with the story of the book of Revelation. In biblical times, Patmos wasn't a

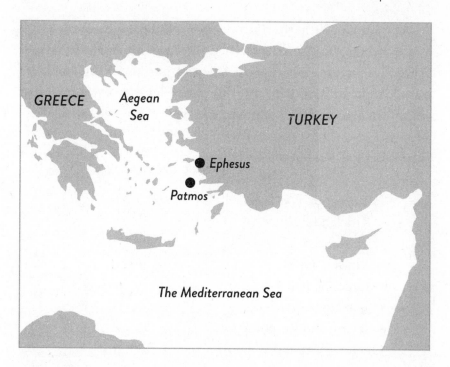

fashionable location. The Romans used it to banish those, like Saint John, whom they wanted to silence or cancel.

As we've already seen, God views the circumstances of life differently than we do, and He chose this small island to reveal His panorama of the future and provide His last surviving apostle with apocalyptic truth about the fifty final events in world history. This is the place God chose to conclude His written revelation—the Scriptures—by revealing the course of earth's dying days.

The first chapter of Revelation serves as a prologue that sets the stage for the entire book and orients us to all that follows. It not only provides the background for the book but also gives us the key for interpreting the symbolism that characterizes the material to follow. If we understand the first chapter, we can correctly interpret the subsequent visions. Chapter 1 is made up of (1) the introduction in verses 1–8 and (2) the opening vision of Christ in verses 9–20.

Let's begin with the introduction of the book—Revelation 1:1–8—which is as simple and concise as any paragraph of Scripture. Packed into these verses are the title and purpose of the book, its transmission, its blessing, a greeting, a doxology (an exclamation of praise), and an opening hymn and response.

### The Prologue of Revelation

1. Introduction (vv. 1–8)
   - Title and Purpose (v. 1)
   - Transmission (vv. 1–2)
   - Blessing (v. 3)
   - Greeting (vv. 4–5)
   - Doxology (vv. 5–6)
   - Hymn and Response (vv. 7–8)
2. Opening Vision (vv. 9–20)

## Title and Purpose

The title of Revelation is given in the first verse: *The revelation from Jesus Christ.* John wrote Revelation in the common language of his day—Greek—and the word *revelation* is translated from the Greek term *apokalypsis,* from which we get our English word *apocalypse.* In Greek, this term doesn't mean "disaster" but "unveiling." The prefix (*apo*) means "from," and the root word means "to hide." So the term actually means "to remove something from hiding, to reveal, to unveil."[2]

My sister and I commissioned our friend Ken Simmelink to create an oil painting of our family home in Roan Mountain, Tennessee. Though the house has been enlarged, it had a humble beginning—a log cabin constructed by hand during World War II for my elderly grandmother. We had some old photographs and a lot of memories, and we wanted people to see it as we remembered it from childhood.

When the painting was finished, we went to Ken's home to view it. He had it sitting on an easel in his living room, covered with a cloth and hidden from view. We took our seats as Ken explained how he had gone about crafting the work and the approach he had taken in creating the image. We could hardly wait until the moment he lifted the covering and revealed the beautiful painting he'd created. We loved it, and it now hangs on the dining room wall in the enlarged cabin.

This moment of Ken revealing his painting shows the meaning of the word *apokalypsis*. God knows exactly what's going to happen in the future. He has already painted the picture, and the history of the world is moving along a preordained route toward its total fulfillment. He knows everything to come, which we could never foresee by our own intuition. In the book of Revelation, God lifts the cloth and shows us His plan for tomorrow.

That leads us to the last half of verse 1, which sums up the book in one phrase and serves as its statement of purpose:

*The revelation from Jesus Christ, which God gave him to show his servants what must soon take place.*

Notice the phrase *his servants*. The information in Revelation isn't for the world, which disregards it. It's for us—for Christ-followers—who value its message and long for our Lord's appearing. It's for those who know Jesus as their Savior and who are eager for details about His return. This is information for the saints, for those who realize they are citizens of heaven traveling through this troubled earth as ambassadors for the King.

Notice the word *must*. The verse says *to show his servants what* must *soon take place*.

The events described in this book are preplanned and preordained by the Author of time and eternity, and they will happen exactly as announced. They *must* happen. No unexpected contingencies can delay or derail them. God's plans are irreversible and unchangeable, inscribed in stone on the walls of His firm and fixed decrees.

Don't overlook the word *soon*—*to show his servants what must soon take place.* Perhaps you're thinking, *But it's been nearly two thousand years since these words were written! That doesn't seem "soon" to me.*

The word *soon* could be translated *quickly, suddenly,* or *swiftly,* indicating these events, once unleashed, will come with sudden force.

It's also true that *soon* is a relative term, and the speaker is the eternal God. To Him, a thousand years are like a day and a day is like a thousand years (2 Peter 3:8). He views the calendar from the perspective of eternity, and to Him a thousand years pass as quickly as a mere day. The book of Revelation is given from God's viewpoint, which means Jesus rose from the dead and ascended to heaven only a couple of days ago, as it were. The interim between our Lord's first and second comings is very brief from the vantage point of eternity. The unfolding of history may not seem "soon" to us, but from God's standpoint things are moving quickly—more quickly now than ever.

God
↓
Jesus
↓
Angel
↓
John
↓
Seven Churches
of Asia
↓
Us
↓
Others

## Transmission

Continuing through verses 1 and 2, we learn the book of Revelation is to be shared, and there's an interesting chain of transmission. It has come to us in a deliberate way. God the Father gave this information to Jesus Christ, who gave it to an angel, who gave it to the apostle John, who wrote it down for seven churches in Asia Minor; and from them it came to us via the inspired Word of God. This indicates it shouldn't stop with us. This is a pass-along book, a pulse-quickening, heart-lifting message to be shared.

## Blessing

Verse 3 continues with a blessing for those who read and study the final pages of the Bible. As I said in the introduction, Revelation is the only book in the Bible with a specific blessing for those who read and heed it. Revelation 1:3 says,

> *Blessed is the one who reads aloud the words of this prophecy, and blessed are those who hear it and take to heart what is written in it, because the time is near.*

A similar blessing occurs near the end of the book too, in Revelation 22:7.

As Dr. W. A. Criswell pointed out, if we are so deeply blessed by the Gospels and strengthened by the message of our Lord's first coming—when He came as a suffering servant and His deity was veiled and He died a torturous death—how much more should we be blessed by contemplating His second coming, His return in power and glory?[3]

*Revelation is the only book in the Bible with a specific blessing for those who read and heed it.*

This is a great encouragement for us. We're often stressed by political pressures and the unfolding events in the news. Our private worlds easily come unraveled. Just today, I realized I had too many demands for an allotted time, and a sense of panic swept over me. Later in the day I was gripped by news of a terrorist attack at an airport I've frequented in the past. We're constantly on edge in this world. But the therapy of studying Revelation is like oil on troubled waters. In times like these we need the blessings of this book and the anticipation of its message. How much better we sleep at night with the sure and certain hope of our Lord's soon return!

## Greeting

Having opened his book with its title, purpose, transmission, and blessing, John then introduced himself with an opening greeting, or salutation, in verses 4–5:

> *John, to the seven churches in the province of Asia: Grace and peace to you from him who is, and who was, and who is to come, and from the seven spirits before his throne, and from Jesus Christ, who is the faithful witness, the firstborn from the dead, and the ruler of the kings of the earth.*

The writer is the apostle John, the author of the fourth gospel. The original recipients of this book were attendees of the churches in Ephesus and other nearby cities along the western coast of modern Turkey. Notice the Trinitarian nature of the greeting John gave. Grace and peace come from:

- God the Father (*him who is, and who was, and who is to come*).
- God the Holy Spirit (*the seven spirits before his throne*).
- God the Son (*Jesus Christ, who is the faithful witness, the firstborn from the dead, and the ruler of the kings of the earth*).

Why is the Holy Spirit referred to as *the seven spirits before his throne*? In Revelation, John frequently used the number seven, indicating completion or perfection. He was referring to the perfection of the Holy Spirit and perhaps thinking of the sevenfold description of the Holy Spirit given in Isaiah 11:1–2, where the Holy Spirit is called the Spirit (1) of the LORD, (2) of wisdom, (3) of understanding, (4) of counsel, (5) of might, (6) of knowledge, and (7) of the fear of the LORD.

Alternately, John may have been thinking of Zechariah 4, which describes a seven-branched golden lampstand, accompanied by the words "'Not by might nor by power, but by my Spirit,' says the LORD Almighty" (v. 6).

Revelation was originally sent to seven churches, which, as we'll see, are described as lampstands. The Holy Spirit was present in all seven congregations—a sevenfold Spirit—representing the fact that He dwells among all churches of the Lord Jesus everywhere on earth. So we have several ways of looking at the Holy Spirit using the number seven—in His perfections, in His attributes, and among His churches.

## Doxology

Verses 5–6 burst into doxology, an exuberant expression of praise:

*To him who loves us and has freed us from our sins by his blood, and has made us to be a kingdom and priests to serve his God and Father—to Him be glory and power for ever and ever! Amen.*

Though exiled on the island of Patmos, John was bursting with praise because God had loved him, freed him from his sins by the blood of Jesus, and included him as part of His kingdom and His priesthood that serves the Lord, to whom belongs glory and power forever and ever. Even when we're exiled by circumstances and stranded on islands of difficulty, we can worship and praise God. That changes our attitudes in every situation. The entire book of Revelation brims with praise and rings with joyful songs of worship.

> **The entire book of Revelation brims with praise and rings with joyful songs of worship.**

## Hymn and Response

The introduction of the book concludes with the first of many hymns in Revelation. In modern translations, we can recognize these hymns by their formatted arrangement in the book. You'll see them indented or centered like a poem or like the lyrics of a song. Verse 7 says,

> *"Look, he is coming with the clouds,"*
> *and "every eye will see him,*
> *even those who pierced him";*
> *and all peoples on earth "will mourn because of him."*
> *So shall it be! Amen.*

How much we can learn about our Lord's return in this short stanza! At the moment of His return, He will descend through dramatic clouds of glory and somehow become visible to everyone on earth and to everyone from human history, including those who crucified Him, wherever they are residing. His coming will anguish those who have rejected Him and thrill those who love Him. And nothing can change the certainty of His return—so shall it be! Amen.

In verse 8, the Lord responded to this hymn, saying, "I am the Alpha and the Omega . . . who is, and who was, and who is to come, the Almighty."

## The Opening Vision

The second part of the prologue of Revelation, which makes up chapter 1, brings us to the opening vision of the book. In verse 9, John paused to introduce himself again, saying,

> *I, John . . . was on the island of Patmos because of the word of God*
> *and the testimony of Jesus.*

In his later years, we believe the apostle John was headquartered in the city of Ephesus and served as the overseer, or bishop, of the churches in that area. Wanting to minimize his influence, Roman authorities banished him to Patmos, probably during the reign of Emperor Domitian, who ruled from AD 81 to 96.[4] Patmos was an island in the Aegean Sea only sixty miles from Ephesus.[5]

John continued in verse 10, saying,

*On the Lord's Day I was in the Spirit.*

Some interpret this as "I was caught up by the Spirit and transported into the visions of the end of the age connected with the Lord's return, that is, the Lord's Day of Judgment." But the simplest understanding is that John was worshiping as a Spirit-filled believer on Sunday when he began receiving this series of visions.

In verse 11, John addressed his readers, members of the seven churches in Asia Minor. As bishop of Ephesus, John probably kept an itinerary and preached regularly in these churches.

Beginning in verse 12, we have the foundational vision of the book—a glimpse of the Lord Jesus Christ as He now appears in all His glory. This was the first time John had seen Jesus since the Lord ascended into heaven sixty or so years before. John now saw Jesus, enthroned, resplendent in glory. I believe this vision contains some literal elements of the present appearance of Christ, though symbolism is overlaid across it. One of the things we should bear in mind while reading Revelation is that an object can be both literal and symbolic at the same time (just as the American flag is, for example).

John said,

*I turned around to see the voice that was speaking to me. And when I turned I saw seven golden lampstands, and among the lampstands was someone like a son of man, dressed in a robe reaching down to*

*his feet and with a golden sash around his chest. The hair on his head
was white like wool, as white as snow, and his eyes were like blazing
fire. His feet were like bronze glowing in a furnace, and his voice was
like the sound of rushing waters. . . . His face was like the sun shining
in all its brilliance.* (vv. 12–16)

Reading those words reminds me of dramatic passages from
earlier books of the Bible. The images in Revelation are consistent
with what we see in many of the Old Testament visions, especially
when God's throne is pictured, often surrounded by angelic beings
of various kinds. Some scholars say John borrowed heavily from Old
Testament passages, and that's true. But perhaps it's better to state
that John was seeing new, original visions. The images were simply
consistent with the ones seen by Daniel, Isaiah, Ezekiel, and others.

What John saw in this vision is remarkably similar to Daniel's
vision of the throne of God in Daniel 7:9–14, which is another
powerful apocalyptic scene related to the last days.

I'm also reminded of Jesus on the Mount of Transfiguration
in Matthew. On that occasion, John, James, and Peter glimpsed
something of our Lord's intrinsic and eternal glory. "There he
was transfigured before them. His face shone like the sun, and his
clothes became as white as the light" (17:2). The disciples saw a
partial manifestation of the essential glory of Jesus.

In his Patmos vision, John saw even more of His glory. He saw the
resplendent Christ walking among seven golden lampstands, which,
according to verse 20, represented the seven churches of Asia.

It's glorious to think that the eternal Ruler of the Universe loves
to walk among us and be present in His churches. When we gather
for worship with other believers, Jesus is there, walking among us
by means of His Holy Spirit. When we labor alongside other believers for the expansion of the gospel, there He is among us; and our
work is done not by might or power but by His Spirit.

As I said, this passage shows how John interpreted the metaphor of the candlesticks, so we don't have to guess about their meaning. The last phrase of the chapter is *and the seven lampstands are the seven churches.* As we'll see, Revelation is a book of symbols, but much of its symbolism is interpreted in the text, so the book isn't as perplexing as it first appears.

*When we gather for worship with other believers, Jesus is there, walking among us by means of His Holy Spirit.*

John's view of Jesus was heart-stopping:

> *When I saw him, I fell at his feet as though dead. Then he placed his right hand on me and said: "Do not be afraid. I am the First and the Last. I am the Living One; I was dead, and now look, I am alive for ever and ever!"* (vv. 17–18)

Jesus opened His book of revelations to us by telling us on the first page about the two responses we should have: (1) don't be afraid and (2) remember Jesus died for us and is now alive—forever!

We don't know what tomorrow's headlines will bring, nor can we anticipate what will befall us today or tomorrow. But one reality overrides everything else—Jesus is alive, so we needn't fear. When He rose from the dead, He overcame every challenge, overthrew every enemy, and overturned every affliction. He stripped away any reason for sleepless nights or fretful days. He set the stage for the righteous consummation of all His intentions and paved the way for the new heaven and new earth.

## The Outline

The prologue of Revelation ends with a simple outline that shows us how the book will unfold. The Lord told John in verse 19,

*Write, therefore, what you have seen, what is now and what will take place later.*

This verse gives us the threefold outline to Revelation.

1. *What you have seen* refers to what John had just seen, the opening vision of the glorified Christ in chapter 1.
2. *What is now* involves the current condition of the seven churches to whom John addressed his book. The seven brief messages to these congregations occupy Revelation 2–3. These messages also speak to us and to our churches now, in the present time.
3. *What will take place later* is the prophetic and predictive portion of Revelation, which presents fifty events that will dramatically conclude the annals of human history and usher in the endless ages of the eternal state. This material spans chapters 4–22.[6]

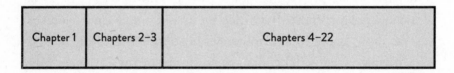

| Chapter 1 | Chapters 2–3 | Chapters 4–22 |
| --- | --- | --- |

Before we go further, let me suggest you read the first chapter of Revelation repeatedly until you have a firm grasp of its simplicity and splendor. Put yourself in John's shoes. Imagine the distress of being exiled to an island far from friends and family, not knowing what will happen to the churches for which you're responsible, not knowing whether the Christian movement will survive the terrible persecutions of Rome.

There, amid all your loneliness and uncertainty, your dearest friend, Jesus, makes a special visit in His resurrected and glorified state, and He tells you, in essence, "Don't be afraid. Remember, I was dead but I'm now alive—and I'm alive forever. Everything will end as I intend, and My intention is to bless you. Let Me give you the details. I'm going to show you what must soon take place. I will unveil the world of tomorrow. I'm going to fill you with hope for the coming days—for both time and eternity."

Jesus was speaking not only to John but to us as well. We have the book of Revelation—all twenty-two wonderful chapters—because we need its message in times like these. How sad to have this book but not study it. How sad to study it but not understand it. How sad to understand it but not obey it.

On the other hand, how wonderful to trust its message, look forward to its fulfillment, and prepare for the sensational events about to engulf the world and lead us into eternity!

# CHAPTER 3

# Christ's Final Messages
## to the Churches
*Revelation 2–3*

I've been going to the same doctor for more than thirty-five years, and after my annual exam I've always thanked him for keeping me healthy another year. His response never varies. He smiles, points upward, and says, "I don't have much to do with it. The good Lord is in charge." Nevertheless, I keep going back to Dr. Gaston because I need someone to periodically evaluate my health, look at my lab results, check my X-rays, listen to my breathing, tap my knee with a hammer, and tell me if anything is wrong.

What if we had an annual appointment with the Great Physician to check the status of our emotional and spiritual health? Or what if He showed up once a year at your church for an annual appraisal of your congregation's fitness and vitality?

That's what happened in Revelation 2–3. Before entrusting the electrifying content of the book of Revelation to the seven churches of Asia, the Lord Jesus wanted to make sure they were as strong and vital as possible. After all, if you had sealed intelligence about the future—prophecy sure, certain, and secret—to whom would you entrust it? The last apostle was nearing the end of his earthly days and the other eleven had already been murdered one by one. The church was in the throes of persecution and the fledgling Christian movement was hanging by a thread. Things seemed bleak, as they do today. But the enthroned Jesus knew the end of the story. He was alive and seated at the right hand of the majesty of heaven, and the times were twisting and turning within the parameters of His providence. History was rolling like a river in channels precut by His divine sovereignty, and He wanted to reveal to His followers the final spasms of the sordid history of humanity. He wanted to show His own people how wonderfully justice would prevail and eternity would win.

Suppose you had all that information ready to reveal. To whom would you entrust it? Jesus Christ was about to commit the final book of His Bible and its coded information about the future to a group of seven ordinary churches peppered along the western coast of Turkey.

*Things seemed bleak, but the enthroned Jesus knew the end of the story. The times were twisting and turning within the parameters of His providence.*

Before lifting the veil from future events and confiding this concluding data to the congregations to whom it was originally addressed, the Lord Jesus wanted to say a few personal words to each church to make it stronger and better equipped to proclaim His final message to the world and to all subsequent ages.

Revelation 2 and 3 contain seven miniature epistles written by Jesus Himself to seven churches under the oversight of the apostle John. These letters are convicting and vital for today's church—literal messages for literal churches.

Each of the seven messages was addressed to the "angel" of the church, but there are two possible interpretations of that word. Perhaps every church has an assigned angel. But the term *angel* comes from the Greek word *angelos*, meaning "messenger."[1] Many commentators believe that in the context of Revelation 2–3, *angelos* refers to the person who read and related the message to the local church—the pastor or elder.[2]

Each of these seven messages follows a general formula. Every

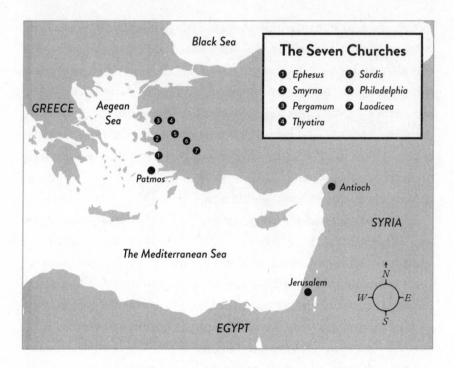

paragraph is addressed to the messenger of the church and includes a description of Christ taken from the vision in chapter 1. In general, each message provides a commendation, gives a rebuke, ends with a promise for those who listen and obey, and admonishes everyone to hear the message.

Despite the similarities, each of the seven notes is specific to the church being addressed. The first church on the list was Ephesus, which was the largest and most prominent church. It was also apparently John's home base.[3] I once joined my son-in-law Joshua on a visit to the ruins of Ephesus, which are so fabulous you could well imagine the apostle Paul walking down the street or the apostle John preaching in the square.

I'm struck by how much of the New Testament was originally addressed to Ephesus. This was the strongest and the leading church in Asia, and it became a sort of headquarters for gospel work in the apostolic era. Paul wrote the book of Ephesians, his loftiest letter, to this congregation. But he also sent the letters we call 1 Timothy and 2 Timothy to Ephesus because, we believe, Timothy was the bishop of that church when those pastoral epistles were written. John's first letter was also probably addressed to this congregation. And finally, we can assume the book of Revelation was first read in the city of Ephesus.

These seven messages to the churches of Asia are perennial in their application. In every age there are congregations like these, and in every church there are Christians who fit the descriptions of these churches. These two chapters are addressed, as it were, to every congregation and to every Christian.

Revelation 2 and 3 are challenging for us to read because they force us to examine ourselves, confess the deep weaknesses of our hearts, and fan into flame the zeal needed to be Last Days People.

> *In every age there are congregations like these, and in every church there are Christians who fit the descriptions of these churches.*

## Revelation 2–3
### Miniature Epistles to the Seven Churches of Asia

**Ephesus**
A Historic Church with a Fading Spirit

**Smyrna**
A Faithful Church in a Hostile Environment

**Pergamum**
A Strategic Church with an Ungodly Faction

**Thyatira**
A Thriving Church with a Cancerous Spot

**Sardis**
A Dead Church with a Godly Remnant

**Philadelphia**
A Feeble Church with an Open Door

**Laodicea**
An Affluent Church with a Lukewarm Faith

**Notes**

These messages represent how the Lord Jesus sees our churches and their members—you and me. The important thing is not how we appear to ourselves or others but how we appear to Him.

There are some of the strengths and weaknesses of these churches in every congregation and in every one of us. These diagnostic evaluations help us make corrections and become the people Jesus wants us to be.

These two chapters represent the two thousand years of Christian history—not necessarily seven different stages of church history, but what the Lord wants His church to be between the ascension and the tribulation.

*Ephesus* is a church that lost its first love. Jesus commended the Ephesians for their hard work, perseverance, doctrinal purity, and zeal, but He warned them about letting the intensity of their love for Him weaken.

In *Smyrna*, the local congregation was facing persecution. Jesus reassured the members of this church that, though they felt poor and afflicted, they were rich. Though they were facing increasing persecution, they should never fear.

The church in *Pergamum* was living in a satanic area, yet they had stayed true to Christ. Some members' faith and morality were eroding, however, and these members needed to repent.

In *Thyatira*, the congregation had allowed a false teacher to minister. Though the church was thriving in its work and maintaining its perseverance, it needed to eject the heretic before they damaged the doctrine and integrity of the entire congregation.

The church in *Sardis* was dying. It appeared to be healthy, but in the eyes of Christ it was in trouble. A minority of members remained passionate and pure, and the Lord appealed to them to strengthen what remained.

In *Philadelphia*, the church had an open door for ministry. The Philadelphians felt weak, but they hadn't given up and Jesus was bringing them new opportunities for ministry.

In *Laodicea*, the church was lukewarm. Hot water is great for beverages and bathing, and cold water is refreshing. But lukewarm water is good for nothing. The Laodiceans were in worse shape than they realized, and their church was in danger of spiritual collapse. Yet there was still time for them to repent and reestablish a vital relationship with Christ.

We can't study these seven brief letters without applying them to our own churches and to our own lives. I've invested over half my life in serving as a local pastor, and I've seen all these tendencies in the churches I've pastored.

I also see them in my own heart.

The Lord wants us to be as sound and strong as possible so we'll handle wisely His information about the future. I've gone through the seven messages myself, and I found it very helpful to list all the faults Jesus saw in the churches and all the strengths for which He commended them. Here is how I jotted it down in my study journal.

*Faults to Avoid*

- letting our love die down (Revelation 2:4)
- tolerating false teachers and their satanic doctrines (2:14–16, 20–25)
- compromising with worldliness (3:16–17)
- sexual immorality (2:14, 20)
- self-deception: thinking we're alive and rich when we're dead and poor (3:1, 17)
- lagging work (3:2)
- lukewarm zeal (3:15–16)

*Qualities to Emulate*

- good deeds, hard work, and faithful service (2:2, 13, 19; 3:8–10)
- love (2:19)
- faith (2:13, 19)
- perseverance and endurance (2:2–3, 13, 19; 3:8, 10)
- rejection of wicked people and false prophets (2:2, 13, 24)
- faithfulness amid persecution (2:3, 10, 13)
- obedience amid weakness (3:8)
- personal purity (3:4–5)
- fellowship with Christ (3:11–12)

Take some time to pore over both lists. Even better, make this a personal project. Read Revelation 2–3 with a pencil or pen, and mark the verses that apply to you most. Do you see yourself anywhere among the weaknesses? Are there growing cracks in your personal holiness? Where are you on the second list? Is there progress in your life for which you can thank the Lord Jesus?

When I first began studying Revelation as a young adult, I skimmed over these chapters because they depressed me. I said to myself, *These churches were a mess! How distressing!* But over the years, I've changed my attitude. There aren't any perfect churches on earth, for all of them are filled with people like you and me who are imperfect. Even so, it's important to face our imperfections and to ask the Lord to continue working in us what is pleasing to Him.

*It's important to face our imperfections and to ask the Lord to continue working in us what is pleasing to Him.*

The psalmist said, "The LORD will perfect that which concerns me; Your mercy, O LORD, endures forever" (Psalm 138:8 NKJV). The apostle Paul told the Philippians, "I always pray with joy . . . being confident of this, that he who began a good work in you will carry it on to completion until the day of Christ Jesus" (Philippians 1:4–6).

My most recent Scripture memory project has been 1 Thessalonians 5:23–24, which says, "May God Himself, the God of peace, sanctify you through and through. May your whole spirit, soul and body be kept blameless at the coming of our Lord Jesus Christ. The one who calls you is faithful, and he will do it."

If we're going to carry the message of Revelation to a world in crisis and persevere with both faith and joy until the end, we need to stay in optimum emotional and spiritual health. This is no time for wobbly Christians or unsound churches. Before we pick up the torch of Revelation 4–22 and race into the world with the messages of Jesus and of judgment, let's visit the Great Physician and let Him infuse us with the glow of inner health that comes from the very bloodstream of Christ.

# CHAPTER 4

# The Foreseeable Future
## *Revelation 4–22*

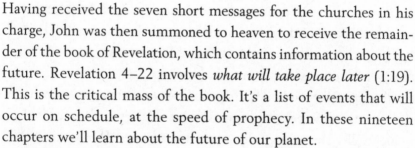

Having received the seven short messages for the churches in his charge, John was then summoned to heaven to receive the remainder of the book of Revelation, which contains information about the future. Revelation 4–22 involves *what will take place later* (1:19). This is the critical mass of the book. It's a list of events that will occur on schedule, at the speed of prophecy. In these nineteen chapters we'll learn about the future of our planet.

There are twenty-one key events, signified by the breaking of seven seals, the blowing of seven trumpets, and the pouring out of seven bowls of wrath. These events are interwoven with twenty-nine other concomitant events, bringing us to a total number of fifty.[1]

Throughout my years of studying the book of Revelation, my primary questions have been, Are the events described in this book sequential? That is, do they unfold in chronological order? Or do they overlap and occur concurrently? Are they linear or do they cycle over one another, each adding more details?

As I said, three series of events make up the heart of the action in Revelation—the seven seals, the seven trumpets, and the seven bowls of wrath. For a long time, I felt these three series overlapped each other, like our old school textbooks with transparent pages describing the human body. If you're my age, you remember those. One page was the skeleton. Across it went a plastic page showing the heart and other organs. Another overlay showed the muscles and flesh, and finally, the skin.

The primary visions in Daniel overlay one another like this, and there is a strong connection between the Old Testament book of Daniel and Revelation. Daniel 2 describes a great statue with four parts, Daniel 7 includes four beasts, and so forth. Each succeeding vision adds more details to the entire picture.

I clung to the suspicion that the seven bowls of wrath added details to the seven trumpets, which were an overlay of the seven seals. There are several variations of this view, especially one that suggests the last seal contains the seven trumpets, and the last trumpet telescopes into the seven bowls of wrath. It can get complicated. I respect those who view the events of Revelation as recapitulating the cycle of events and appreciate this approach.

But upon further study and reflection over time, I've concluded the events of Revelation can be best understood as unfolding sequentially, chronologically, one after another. In my view, they represent fifty events that will occur in succession. They are concatenated. Like falling dominoes, each of these events will trigger the next. Taken together, they will terminate human history, lead to the return of Christ, and eventually usher in the eternal state. When we read the book from that perspective, it unfurls like a scroll.

The phrase *after this* occurs over and over in Revelation 4–22, implying a logical progression of the action. Ditto the similar word *then*, which shows up fifty-four times to move the action forward from step to step.

And yet the events do cycle over one another in this sense: each succeeding series is a stronger version of the one that came before it. The bowls of wrath are like the trumpets, only worse. The trumpets are like the seals, only worse. There is a pattern that intensifies and deepens as we progress through the tribulation, and there are parallels between the three series.

I encourage you to look at Revelation in this way. As you further study this book in the future, you may want to view these lists as occurring concurrently or telescopically, or interpret some items as parentheses or flashbacks. It won't affect the reality of the events, just the order in which they occur.

Nevertheless and without being dogmatic, it seems reasonably clear to me the most natural way to understand and to teach this book is by listing the events as they occur in the text, one after the other, seeing within them overlapping patterns. In this way, you can read through the book of Revelation in your own Bible and number each event in the margin. You'll find that the entire book opens up to you.

I also believe this represents the most natural way most people would read the book. Scholars can bore deeply into the background of each scene and develop systems, but most of us aren't scholars. The Bible was written to be understood by ordinary and everyday Christians. If my inclination is true—that the events in Revelation are a straightforward and sequential record of coming events—I think I can help even children grasp the flow of the future as it unfolds here.

Let's begin with a broad overview of our remaining chapters. Like I've already said, Revelation 4–22 pertains to the future, to events that have not yet occurred. This section of the book has a simple plan.

- Chapters 4–5 describe the heavenly celebration and courtyard drama that will launch God's judgment of evil and the seven years of tribulation.
- Chapters 6–18 describe these seven years of coming tribulation through three series of catastrophic events—the

seven seals, the seven trumpets, and the seven bowls of wrath.

- Chapter 19 describes the glorious return of Christ, who will put an end to the tribulation.
- Chapter 20 describes the thousand-year reign of Christ and the great white throne judgment.
- Chapters 21–22 describe the new heaven and the new earth—our eternal home.

OVERVIEW OF CHAPTERS 4–22

| Opening Celebration in Heaven | The Tribulation | The Return of Christ | The Millennium | The New Heaven and Earth |
|---|---|---|---|---|
| Chapters 4–5 | Chapters 6–18 | Chapter 19 | Chapter 20 | Chapters 21–22 |

Truly, the broad contents of Revelation are as simple as that. Now, turn the page and let's begin our study of the fifty final events in world history as they uncoil in Revelation 4–22.

PART 2

# THE FIFTY FINAL EVENTS

*Revelation 4–22*

# The First Half of the Tribulation

## Revelation 4–11

Revelation 4–11 covers the first three and a half years of the seven years of tribulation predicted by Daniel and Jesus.

- In Matthew 24:21 Jesus said, "Then there will be great distress, unequaled from the beginning of the world until now—and never to be equaled again."
- Daniel 9:27 (TLB) says, "This king [the Antichrist] will make a seven-year treaty with the people [the nation of Israel], but after half that time, he will break his pledge and stop the Jews from all their sacrifices and their offerings; then, as a climax to all his terrible deeds, the Enemy shall utterly defile the sanctuary of God. But in God's time and plan, his judgment will be poured out upon this Evil One."

Revelation 4–18 gives us a detailed explanation of this entire seven-year period when a lawless ruler will rise to power, the world will be in chaos, sin will be judged, people will have a final opportunity to repent and turn to Christ, and the drama will build for the return of Christ.

Some global cataclysm will shake humanity to its core, triggering the development of a one-world government. A powerful global ruler will emerge and, through armed conflict, come to dominate world affairs. He will establish a treaty with Israel. The world will be in turmoil during these forty-two months and nations will violently jockey for position, but Israel will be secure and will rebuild its historic temple before or during this time.

This is what we'll see in Revelation 4–11. And it all begins with a vast scene in the cosmic heavens (Revelation 4–5) as God convenes His council and launches final events in world history.

## The Tribulation

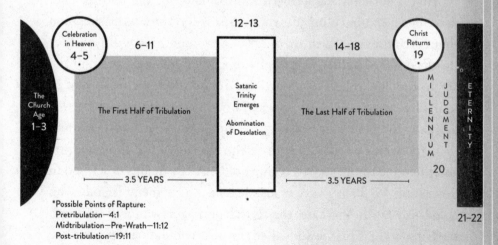

The Church Age 1–3

Celebration in Heaven 4–5

6–11

The First Half of Tribulation

3.5 YEARS

12–13

Satanic Trinity Emerges

Abomination of Desolation

14–18

The Last Half of Tribulation

3.5 YEARS

Christ Returns 19

MILLENNIUM

JUDGMENT 20

ETERNITY

21–22

*Possible Points of Rapture:
Pretribulation—4:1
Midtribulation—Pre-Wrath—11:12
Post-tribulation—19:11

# The Potential Rapture
# of the Church (4:1)

What an opening scene! The prophetic portion of Revelation starts with these words from John:

> *After this I looked, and there before me was a door standing open in heaven. And the voice I had first heard speaking to me like a trumpet said, "Come up here, and I will show you what must take place after this." (4:1)*

At this point in the book, John was caught up in some way to heaven to learn what will take place "after this," that is, after the age of the church, which is described in chapters 2–3. My working theory suggests Revelation 4:1 could indicate the rapture ("catching up") of the entire church. The language of rapture is in this verse: the doorway to heaven is opened, a voice speaks like a trumpet, and the words *Come up here* are spoken.

In 1 Thessalonians 4 and 1 Corinthians 15, the apostle Paul described a coming moment when Jesus will return in the skies and shout a command. With the blast of a trumpet, He will resurrect the dead saints and rapture the living church, meeting them in the air. In the book of Revelation, John did not describe this event in terms like we see in Paul's letters. So we have to decide where this dramatic moment best fits in the sequence of events in Revelation.

An obvious possibility is this: The rapture of the church is one and the same as the second coming of Christ, which is described in Revelation 19. That's very plausible, and I have many friends who hold this view. In this case, the church of that era would go through the tribulation. This view is called the post-tribulation rapture since it occurs after the tribulation at the moment of Christ's return.

Others believe the rapture of the church will occur sometime near the middle of the tribulation or just before the unfolding of the wrath of God as revealed in the seven bowls of wrath, which will be poured out during the final three and a half years. Still others are inclined to my working theory, that the church will be raptured before the tribulation begins, which means the wording of Revelation 4:1 is emblematic of the rapture. This is the pre-tribulation view of the rapture.[1]

I have no doubt the resurrection and the rapture are true and coming events—it's our glorious hope! I'm not dogmatic about where we place it in the sequence of events in Revelation (hence my adjective *potential* above, in the title of this event). But it does seem logical to me to put it here at the beginning of chapter 4. This is immediately after the message to the seven churches, which is our Lord's final words to the entire church of all ages.

Interestingly, the church disappears from the pages of Revelation after this, as the redemptive action of God shifts back to the nation of Israel. My dad, who was a keen student of prophecy, was always amazed at the rebirth of the modern state of Israel during his lifetime, in 1948. He felt it somehow triggered a countdown toward the tribulation, and I agree. The Lord is not finished with Israel. Just as this tiny nation was instrumental in the first coming of Christ, so it will be instrumental in the second coming—hence, Satan's savage and repeated attempts to destroy the Jewish people.

> *The Lord is not finished with Israel. Just as this tiny nation was instrumental in the first coming of Christ, so it will be instrumental in the second coming.*

Furthermore, in 2 Thessalonians 2:6–7, Paul indicated that something or someone would be removed before the Antichrist would be revealed, and in Revelation 3:10, Jesus told one of the churches, *I will also keep you from the hour of trial that is going to come on the whole world.*

37

Placing the rapture at Revelation 4:1 also makes possible our belief in the imminence of Christ's return—He may come for us at any moment. If so, He will come and remove His church before the onset of the tribulation. The sudden disappearance of billions of people on earth could easily lead to the kind of global emergency that would trigger the remaining events in Revelation.

I respect the opinions of those who hold various views on the timing of the rapture and cannot be dogmatic about my own.

## The Tribulation

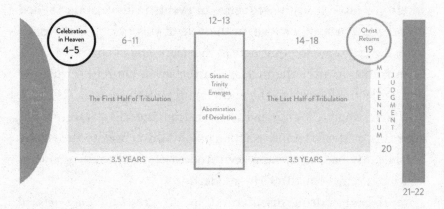

---

EVENT 2

# Celebration Erupts in Heaven (4:2–5:14)

The text continues:

> *At once I was in the Spirit, and there before me was a throne in heaven with someone sitting on it. And the one who sat there had the appearance of jasper and ruby. A rainbow that shone like an emerald encircled the throne.* (4:2–3)

As John arrived in heaven, he saw and heard a great worship service in progress. Imagine walking down a city street on a hot summer's evening and passing a church, its windows and doors open. You can glimpse the action on the inside. You can hear the singing, see the worshipers, get a glimpse of those on the platform, and feel the exuberance of those in attendance. You may even ascend the steps and peer in the door. That's what we're allowed to do in Revelation 4–5. We can peer through the door and watch a dramatic worship experience at the heart of heaven.

Everything in this passage centers on the throne of Almighty God. The word *throne* occurs thirty-eight times in Revelation and sixteen times in these two chapters! The subject of God's heavenly throne is one of the most fascinating and thrilling subjects in Scripture. God's seat of power is described several times in the Bible, in places like Isaiah 6 and Ezekiel 1. The descriptions are consistent and enable us to visualize it to the extent we possibly can. I often imagine the great throne of God somewhere above my head beyond the dome of earth's atmosphere, occupied by the Sovereign Father, Son, and Holy Spirit, who alone are worthy of worship.

This is also a courtroom scene, very similar to the one described in Daniel 7:9–14. Real business is about to take place here at the throne in Revelation 4. Decisions about judgment will be rendered. But the great emotions are worshipful.

The word *jasper* in this text doesn't refer to the opaque stone known by that name today, but to a crystal that reflects light and sparkles with beauty.[2] It's most likely a reference to a stone like a diamond.[3] So try to imagine it as described—a vast throne, and from its center a brilliant light sparkling like a diamond with shards of ruby-red refractions, and around it a brilliant rainbow, which is the biblical symbol for mercy. The one seated on the throne is God the Father, the first person of the Trinity.

*Surrounding the throne were twenty-four other thrones, and seated on them were twenty-four elders. They were dressed in white and had crowns of gold on their head.* (Revelation 4:4)

The identity of the elders isn't given to us, but I take them to be the redeemed of all the ages, represented by the twelve patriarchs of Israel and the twelve apostles of Jesus. They aren't beside the throne on the left or right, or before the throne. They surround the throne like a dazzling circle. This implies positions of authority.

Some scholars suggest the twenty-four elders are a category of angels. The important thing is the exuberance of their worship and their participation in the unfolding proceedings.

The next verse says,

*In front of the throne, seven lamps were blazing. These are the seven spirits of God.* (v. 5)

As we saw earlier, this is a reference to the Holy Spirit, the third person of the Trinity.

Verse 6 says that in front of the throne was something like a "sea of glass." This is the vast foundational pavement on which the throne sits. Other biblical writers saw the same. It was first spotted by Moses and the seventy elders of Israel in Exodus 24:10, when they "saw the God of Israel. Under his feet was something like a pavement made of lapis lazuli, as bright blue as the sky." In that case, the diamond-like clarity of the "sea of glass" reflected the tone of the sky, giving it a sheen of lapis lazuli blue.

John went on to describe *four living creatures,* or the cherubim, which are supernatural beings who surround the throne and lead in worship (v. 7). They were singing, *Holy, holy, holy is the Lord God Almighty, who was, and is, and is to come* (v. 8).[4]

Verses 9–11 describe the enthusiasm of the worship around God's shimmering throne:

*Whenever the living creatures give glory, honor and thanks to him
who sits on the throne and who lives for ever and ever, the twenty-four
elders fall down before him who sits on the throne and worship him
who lives for ever and ever. They lay their crowns before the throne
and say: "You are worthy, our Lord and God, to receive glory and
honor and power, for you created all things, and by your will they
were created and have their being."*

At the beginning of chapter 5, God the Father holds out a scroll
sealed with seven seals. If you've ever received a letter with a wax
seal on the envelope, you know something of how this looks. In
ancient times, scrolls were rolled up, and a piece of hot wax was
attached to the edge of the roll to secure it. This scroll had seven
such seals.

What does this scroll represent? We don't know. The content
of the scroll is never actually revealed in the book of Revelation, so
we can't be too certain about it.

Some Bible teachers believe this is the Lamb's Book of Life,
which is mentioned elsewhere in Revelation. If so, it would contain
the names of all those redeemed from the beginning of the world.
Their glorious final eternal state in the new heaven and new earth
cannot begin until certain events happen on earth.

Or perhaps this scroll contains the battle plan for the end of
history as we read in Daniel 12:4–9. In military terminology we
have the phrase *sealed orders*. Sealed orders are given to the commander of a ship or squadron, and they are not allowed to open
them until they have proceeded to a certain point into the high seas.

In Daniel 12, we read that the battle plan for the end of history was sealed until the proper time. Now the time has come.

> "But you, Daniel, roll up and seal the words of the scroll until the time of the end. Many will go here and there to increase knowledge."
>
> Then I, Daniel, looked, and there before me stood two others, one on this bank of the river and one on the opposite bank. One of them said to the man clothed in linen, who was above the waters of the river, "How long will it be before these astonishing things are fulfilled?"
>
> The man clothed in linen, who was above the waters of the river, lifted his right hand and his left hand toward heaven, and I heard him swear by him who lives forever, saying, "It will be for a time, times and half a time [three and a half years]. When the power of the holy people has been finally broken, all these things will be completed."
>
> I heard, but I did not understand. So I asked, "My lord, what will the outcome of all this be?"
>
> He replied, "Go your way, Daniel, because the words are rolled up and sealed until the time of the end." (Daniel 12:4–9)

In Revelation 5:2, a mighty angel proclaimed in a loud voice,

*Who is worthy to break the seals and open the scroll?*

No one stepped forward. No one can be found good enough, pure enough, and powerful enough to break the seals and unleash the future. This affected John very deeply, and in the drama of the moment he broke down weeping.

Someone crucial was missing from this awesome scene. In chapter 4, we have God the Father on the throne and the Holy Spirit hovering around the throne. But where is Jesus Christ—the second person of the Trinity, the Lion of the tribe of Judah?

Suddenly John saw Him!

*Then I saw a Lamb, looking as if it had been slain, standing at the center of the throne, encircled by the four living creatures and the elders.* (5:6)

The Lion is a Lamb! This is heaven's way of picturing the two comings of Christ. Our Lord came the first time as a Lamb to be sacrificed for sin. He will come again as a Lion to rule and to reign.

The image of the lamb is the most poignant symbol for Christ in the Bible. It arguably goes all the way back to the garden of Eden, when God slayed an animal to cover the shame of Adam and Eve (Genesis 3:21). In Genesis 4, Abel brought a lamb to God as an offering to the Lord. Abraham offered a ram to the Lord in Genesis 22, and the children of Israel painted their doorposts with the blood of the Passover lambs in Exodus 12.

The prophet Isaiah described the coming Messiah as a sacrificial lamb in Isaiah 53, and John the Baptist introduced Jesus to the nation of Israel, saying, "Look, the Lamb of God, who takes away the sin of the world!" (John 1:29). The apostle Peter wrote, "You were redeemed . . . with the precious blood of Christ, a lamb without blemish or defect" (1 Peter 1:18–19).

*The lamb motif is a crimson ribbon that runs from the garden of Eden to the Celestial City.*

The book of Revelation consummates Christ's redemptive work for eternity, so it's no surprise to find Him pictured as a lamb nearly thirty times in this book. The lamb motif is a crimson ribbon that runs from the garden of Eden to the Celestial City.

What is Jesus about to do? Something no one else can. The Father cannot. The Spirit cannot. The angels cannot. No other human being in history can do what Jesus is about to do—bring to complete fulfillment the saving of His people. He alone bled, died, and rose again to provide redemption. He alone has the righteous blood-bought qualifications to consummate that redemption by beginning the final stage of human history. He alone is the God-Man, the Redeemer, the Judge, the Risen One.

As the Lord Jesus approached God the Father and took the scroll, heaven burst into worship. Revelation 5:11–14 is so beautiful that I spent some time last year memorizing it:

*Then I looked and heard the voice of many angels, numbering thousands upon thousands, and ten thousand times ten thousand. They encircled the throne and the living creatures and the elders. In a loud voice they were saying: "Worthy is the Lamb, who was slain, to receive power and wealth and wisdom and strength and honor and glory and praise!" Then I heard every creature in heaven and on earth and under the earth and on the sea, and all that is in them, saying: "To him who sits on the throne and to the Lamb be praise and honor and glory and power for ever and ever!" The four living creatures said, "Amen," and the elders fell down and worshiped.*

Imagine the scene! A glorious throne sparkling like a diamond with hues of deepest red, encircled by a rainbow and sitting on a vast crystal pavement. Hovering around it are the cherubim, shouting, "Holy, holy, holy!" The twenty-four elders are sitting around the throne, surrounded by millions of angels. The roar of praise is deafening and all of heaven is bursting in praise to the Father and Son and Holy Spirit.

Why are they celebrating?

The moment has come for evil to be judged during a new and swift phase of history, setting the stage for the final events leading to the return of Christ and the dawning of glorious eternity.

This great worship service and throne room drama hasn't actually occurred yet. John saw it prophetically in a vision. He received a glorious preview of the greatest celebration of worship found in

Scripture. This is the convocation that will launch the tribulation. And that leads us to event number 3.

# The Lamb Inaugurates the Tribulation—Seal 1 (6:1)

As John watched, the Lamb opened the first of the seven seals. In other words, Jesus, as it were, slid His finger beneath the edge of the scroll and loosened the first seal. In my opinion, there will be a global emergency that will trigger a worldwide panic. Our imaginations needn't wander far to envision such a time. Certainly something will occur on earth that will launch the tribulation—and this is the moment when the seven years of tribulation begin. The word *tribulation* means "trouble,"[5] and the Bible repeatedly warns that the final years of earth will be the most violent, fierce, and anxious in all history.

The prophet Daniel called it "a time of distress such as has not happened from the beginning of nations until then" (Daniel 12:1).

## The Tribulation

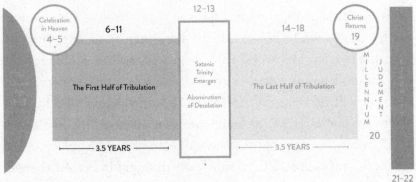

45

The prophet Isaiah said that during these days, the heavens will tremble and the earth will shake from its place "at the wrath of the LORD Almighty" (Isaiah 13:13).

The apostle Paul said that during these days, "Satan . . . will use all sorts of displays of power through signs and wonders that serve the lie" (2 Thessalonians 2:9).

Jesus said, "Those will be days of distress unequalled from the beginning, when God created the world, until now—and never to be equaled again" (Mark 13:19).

EVENT 4

# A Powerful Political Leader Appears (6:1–2)

As Jesus unfastened the first four seals on the mysterious scroll, John saw four horses come galloping toward him. These have been called "the four horsemen of the apocalypse." The first horse was white—the kind ridden by a conqueror. Revelation 6:2 says,

> *Its rider held a bow, and he was given a crown, and he rode out as a conqueror bent on conquest.*

In Revelation 19, the Lord Jesus is symbolized as returning to earth riding a white horse, but the horseman in chapter 6 is not Christ. He is an evil world ruler who will, by the middle of the tribulation, become Satan-possessed and filled with supernatural evil. He will become the Antichrist. I do not know who he is or where he comes from, although we may have a hint in Ezekiel 38:15, where we are told that he will come from his "place in the far north," meaning north of Israel, which might indicate Lebanon, Syria, Turkey, Ukraine, or Russia.

The "far north" could also refer to the supposed home of the false god Baal, who, in ancient Middle Eastern literature,[6] held counsel on a mountain north of Israel and marshaled demonic forces against Zion. Israel's worst enemies had usually invaded from the north. According to scholar Michael Heiser, "A supernatural enemy in the end times would be expected to come from the seat of Baal's authority—the supernatural underworld realm of the dead, in the heights of the north."[7]

This emerging leader will apparently use the aforementioned global crisis as the opportunity to attempt to seize the reins of world domination.

This no longer seems far-fetched. Recent crises have sparked louder calls for globalism. Many elite pundits believe that over-arching worldwide regulatory systems would superintend the world much better than today's nationalism and collection of nation-states. These leaders are calling for globally coordinated strategies to respond to climate change, global equity, universal trade and labor practices, an interconnected economy, and a multilateral approach to conflict. It seems to make sense until one contemplates

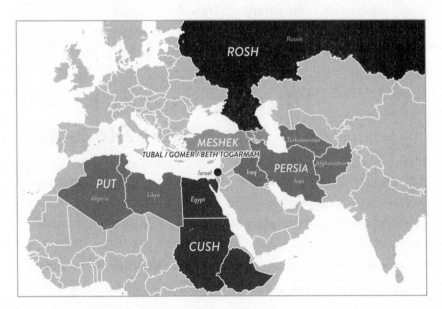

the prospects of this global system falling into anti-biblical and totalitarian hands, which is exactly what will happen.

This global emergency—the disappearance of billions of people at the rapture of the church, a crisis in the Middle East, a worldwide economic collapse and depression, a global technology breakdown or environmental disaster, a lethal pandemic, or simply a series of converging crises from every direction—will set the stage for this popular, powerful, charismatic individual to attempt to become a global dictator.

This ruler will have to fight for domination, so he is seen as holding a weapon and charging into global warfare seeking to conquer every nation that opposes him.

Someone asked me the other day when I thought these events would begin. We don't have dates given to us in Scripture, but we can look at world events. How close are we to an existential global emergency that would trigger the emergence of a one-world government? For the first time since antiquity, we can imagine doomsday scenarios (including weapons of mass destruction, biological weapons, and the threat of uncontrolled technology) that could precipitate such a state of affairs.[8]

EVENT 5

# Global Conflict Rocks the World—Seal 2 (6:3-4)

The emergence of a would-be world dictator leads to a period of global conflict, as we see when Jesus unclasped the second seal. Another horse appeared—a fiery red one. Revelation 6:4 says,

> *Its rider was given power to take peace from the earth and to make people kill each other. To him was given a large sword.*

All over the world, armies will mobilize. Weapons systems will activate. Diplomats will dash and dart from capital to capital like rats on a ship. Wars and rumors of wars will rock the planet. Whole nations will enter into armed conflict as the warrior on the white horse seeks to become the leader of a one-world government.

In His sermon on the end times, Jesus said, "Watch out that no one deceives you. For many will come in my name, claiming, 'I am the Messiah,' and will deceive many. You will hear of wars and rumors of wars, but see to it that you are not alarmed. Nation will rise against nation, and kingdom against kingdom" (Matthew 24:4–7).

Now notice the next words Jesus said in Matthew 24:7: "There will be famines . . . in various places." That's exactly what happens next in Revelation 6.

EVENT 6

# Famine Ravages the Earth—Seal 3 (6:5–6)

In Revelation 6:5, Jesus broke the third seal, and John saw a third horse before him—a black horse whose rider was holding a pair of scales in his hand, the kind that were used in markets for measuring grain. Verse 6 says,

> *Then I heard what sounded like a voice among the four living creatures, saying, "Two pounds of wheat for a day's wages, and six pounds of barley for a day's wage, and do not damage the oil and the wine!"*

The price of wheat and barley will skyrocket. In other words, there will be a shortage of the staples of life like bread. But the warfare and famine will eventually diminish as the global leader assumes more control.

Warfare almost always leads to famine. The United Nations Security Council recently passed a resolution condemning the use of food insecurity and starvation as a tactic of war. In commenting on this, *National Geographic* said, "Wars are inherently violent and harmful, but destruction of resources can sometimes create more catastrophic harm than bombs and bullets. . . . Armed conflict can certainly bring about dangerous conditions of food insecurity."[9]

Notice, however, that the oil and wine will be unaffected. Perhaps that's because the harvest time for olives and grapes is later than that of wheat and barley. If so, this famine will perhaps afflict the world for six or so months before the world leader can reestablish supply routes and stabilize food prices.

EVENT 7

# The Death Rate Soars—
# Seal 4 (6:7–8)

When Jesus opened the fourth seal, John saw a pale horse gallop past him, and its rider's name was Death. Revelation 6:8 tells us that over a fourth of the population of the earth will perish during this season of warfare and its aftermath. In today's terms, that means nearly two billion people will die during the first five or six months of world war.

Now let me circle back to something I said earlier. According to Daniel 9:27, at some point early in these conflicts, the emerging world dictator will ink a peace treaty with the nation of Israel, guaranteeing peace for the Jewish state for seven years. Remember that the nation of Israel was lost to history until 1948. After nearly two thousand years of nonexistence, suddenly the Jewish state was back in its ancestral land.

The verse goes on to say he will break his covenant in the middle of this period by setting up "an abomination that causes desolation," which we later learn is his own image in the temple. Having dominated the world, he will demand the Jewish people worship him too. That will trigger the last half of the tribulation. But for now, this powerful figure will rise in history, begin to dominate the headlines, consolidate his empire, and fight for global dominance. He will make peace with Israel, but the rest of the world will be engulfed in chaos.

So far, everything we've read is plausible. We can follow the trajectory of current events and see how these things could unfold. In Revelation 4, John was caught up to heaven where he witnessed a heavenly convocation of worship and where the scroll containing the battle plan for the last seven years was handed to Jesus Christ. As the Lord broke open the seven seals in heaven, one after the other, events began to transpire on earth—the emerging of a dictator intent on world conquest, global warfare, several months of severe famine, and the death of a quarter of the population of earth.

In the midst of all this, the Jewish state will sign a peace treaty with this man, whom they must regard at this point as a political savior. As the world is gripped by great distress, the land of Israel will enjoy relative safety. I further believe during this time the Jewish people will quickly move to rebuild the Jewish temple on the Temple Mount in Jerusalem, which we will see a bit later.

At the very center of the geopolitical conflicts, then, will be the nation of Israel, back from the dead, as it were, since 1948.

None of this is implausible. The famous physicist Stephen Hawking said that without a "world government," technology could wipe out humanity. Hawking said the dangers of our technology are so great that only a world government can save the human race. But he also fretted that a world government "might become a tyranny."[10]

As I said earlier, globalization is driving much of today's politics and diplomacy. Given the right circumstances, a one-world government could emerge. A sustained existential crisis to the planet could well lead to a global government and an ultimate dictator.

# Multitudes Die for Christ—Seal 5 (6:9–11)

When Jesus opened the fifth seal, John glimpsed a scene that must have surprised him as much as it does us. Revelation 6:9–10 says,

> *When he opened the fifth seal, I saw under the altar the souls of those who had been slain because of the word of God and the testimony they had maintained. They called out in a loud voice, "How long, Sovereign Lord, holy and true, until you judge the inhabitants of the earth and avenge our blood?"*

They were told it would be *a little longer, until the full number of their fellow servants, their brothers and sisters, were killed just as they had been* (v. 11).

The meaning seems relatively clear. During these several months of global conflict, multitudes of people will turn to the Lord Jesus Christ. This must be the greatest revival in the history of the world. If the church is raptured before the tribulation, the sudden shock of the event (along with all the Bibles, sermons, books, videos, and literature left behind) will lead millions to Christ. If the church is still on earth, its witness will be effective during these days of tribulation. But the enemies of the gospel—including the emerging global dictator—will try to eradicate the new believers. This will surely be the worst bloodbath of persecution in the history of the gospel.

The fifth seal implies a tremendous spread of the gospel during the first phases of the tribulation and clearly pictures a terrible time of increased persecution and martyrdom.

Jesus said as much in Matthew 24. Listen again to His words: "You will hear of wars and rumors of wars. . . . There will be famines. . . . All these are the beginning of birth pains. Then you will be handed over to be persecuted and put to death, and you will be hated by all nations because of me" (vv. 6–9).

Jesus also said that in the middle of all these events, there would be "earthquakes in various places" (Matthew 24:7). And that's what we see next.

EVENT 9

# Natural Catastrophes Sweep the Planet—Seal 6 (6:12–17)

In Revelation 6:12–13, Jesus opened the sixth seal.

*There was a great earthquake. The sun turned black like sackcloth made of goat hair, the whole moon turned blood red, and the stars in the sky fell to earth.*

This period of time ends with a series of natural catastrophes in earth and sky, precursors to the coming end of the world as we know it. There will be earthquakes and phenomena in the heavens. Perhaps as a result of volcanic eruptions or nuclear fallout, the sky will darken, sunshine will be dimmed, the moon will take on a ghastly red color, and the stars will regress. It's interesting to recall that John wrote this shortly after the major eruption of Mount Vesuvius, an event seared on the minds of his readers.

One commentator wrote, "All events pictured with the opening of the sixth seal are perfectly consistent with conditions that may well exist early in the tribulation period and yet leave enormous devastation yet to come in the remaining sets of judgments to be revealed."[11]

These cataclysms will terrify even the kings, generals, and wealthy, and everyone will understand that the day of the Lamb's wrath is beginning. These are preshocks and strong foreshadowings of the ultimate natural catastrophes that will accompany the actual return of Christ, which is perhaps six or so years away.

The purpose of all these things isn't just to judge evil; it's also to shake people into an awareness of their need for the gospel. So now, after the sixth seal, something very special happens. The Lord commissions 144,000 Jewish evangelists to fan out over the damaged earth and proclaim the message of Jesus.

EVENT 10

# 144,000 Jewish Evangelists Are Commissioned (7:1–8)

Revelation 7 begins with the phrase *After this.*

That is, "after the first six seals have been opened"—notice the sequential nature of the events. After the sixth seal, John saw four angels putting a halt to the action until God could commission an army of Jewish preachers. John heard their number—144,000—and he learned there were 12,000 from each of the twelve tribes of Israel. These are Jewish evangelists! In the Old Testament, the nation of Israel was composed of twelve tribes that descended from the twelve sons of Jacob, the grandson of Abraham.

In 722 BC, the northern ten tribes had become lost to history when they were defeated and displaced by the Assyrian Empire. After the destruction of the Jewish state by Rome in AD 70, most of the other Jewish families lost their ancestral records. But the omniscient Lord knows everyone's family tree, and now He chooses 12,000 from each of the twelve tribes.[12]

These are new messianic believers, and they are sealed. Being *sealed* is common New Testament language; the moment that we receive Jesus Christ as our Savior, we are sealed and secured in Christ by the Holy Spirit (2 Corinthians 1:22; Ephesians 1:13; 4:30). So here in Revelation 7, we have a group of Jewish people who are gloriously saved amid all the turmoil on earth. Does this seal refer to the Holy Spirit's anointing, or is it a visible mark or sign? I don't know. It's said to be on their foreheads, but we aren't given any details. Yet it will be as though the apostle Paul had been cloned 144,000 times and sent out to every corner of earth in the power of the Holy Spirit to evangelize the globe.

This doesn't mean the entire nation of Israel will be saved and redeemed at this moment. That will happen at the end of the tribulation. These are the firstfruits of the coming conversion of the nation of Israel. These 144,000 evangelists will cover the globe and preach to the nations. As a result, even more people will be saved during the tribulation, though the emerging world dictator and his forces will hunt down and kill many of these new converts. Millions will die from violent persecution and martyrdom, and it will all happen quickly. That's the next item on the list—yet more martyrs arrive in heaven.

EVENT 11

# More Martyrs Arrive in Heaven (7:9–17)

Revelation 7:9 says,

*After this I looked, and there before me was a great multitude that*

*no one could count, from every nation, tribe, people and language,*
*standing before the throne and before the Lamb.*

As the angels look on, these new arrivals in heaven are praising
God for their salvation. For these newly converted martyrs, the
tribulation has become a testimony. Imagine it! On earth a teenage
boy comes to Christ; an elderly grandfather is converted; an entire
family receives the gospel. Then their lives are cut short. They're
shot or stabbed or destroyed in some terrible way. But these people
will instantly be transported to Glory. Here we see them singing
and praising God before His throne.

To make sure we don't misinterpret who they are, we're told
plainly in verse 14,

*These are they who have come out of the great tribulation; they have*
*washed their robes and made them white in the blood of the Lamb.*

The last half of the seven-year period is a time of great tribulation for the nation of Israel, but that hasn't yet begun. Nevertheless,
the entire seven years represent great tribulation for the world. By
this time, perhaps we're two or so years into the seven-year span.

These martyrs who come to Christ during this time—many
undoubtedly as a result of the 144,000 preachers—are highly
blessed:

*They are before the throne of God and serve him day and night in*
*his temple; and he who sits on the throne will shelter them with his*
*presence. "Never again will they hunger; never again will they thirst.*
*The sun will not beat down on them," nor any scorching heat. For the*
*Lamb at the center of the throne will be their shepherd; "he will lead*
*them to springs of living water." "And God will wipe away every tear*
*from their eyes." (7:15–17)*

Like the other items we've studied, this is not far-fetched. The global persecution of Christians today is a scandal of our times, and the media doesn't report enough about it. I follow the ministry of Open Doors, which tracks the persecution of believers around the globe and seeks to minister to them. According to their research, 340 million Christians now live in places where they experience high levels of persecution and discrimination. That's one in eight Christians on earth.[13]

*The global persecution of Christians today is a scandal of our times, and the media doesn't report enough about it.*

The most anti-Christian nation on earth is North Korea, which already functions like a great tribulation state. Anyone discovered as a Christian is killed on the spot or deported to a concentration camp. Afghanistan, Pakistan, Somalia, the Islamic states of North Africa, and some of the Gulf states are deadly for believers. Because of rising Hindu extremism, India has become a dangerous place for believers.[14] Christianity is on the verge of disappearing in Iraq and Syria.[15] In Eritrea, Christians are sometimes held in shipping containers in scorching weather.[16]

Millions of Christians in China are under increasing video and technological surveillance.[17] China has advanced facial recognition software and tracking systems for cell phones, and it monitors its citizens. Facial recognition software is currently being installed in all state-run religious venues, with the data going to government agencies that can withhold social services to those who attend. China is also exporting its artificial intelligence surveillance technologies to many other nations, including many intent on persecuting Christians.[18]

The first years of the tribulation look a lot like modern days, only greatly intensified—globalism, war, famine, death, evangelism, persecution, and martyrdom.

# Dramatic Manifestation of Answered Prayer—Seal 7 (8:1–5)

In Revelation 8, the Lamb opened the seventh seal, and there was silence in heaven for half an hour. In keeping with my general principles for approaching this book, I take this as literal. There's no indication it's a symbol of some sort. Just a verse before, heaven was ringing with praises and filled with songs. But suddenly the Lamb opened the seventh seal, and everyone abruptly ended their songs to see what would happen.

Silence is appropriate when something of grave consequence is about to happen. This is like the silence in a courtroom before the sentence is spoken. It is a silence of intense and reverent suspense. The saints and angels of heaven stood in silence to see what was about to happen next. All eyes were on the next phase of earth's future.

This must be the only time in history when heaven is silent, except for the death of Jesus on the cross. Until now in the book of Revelation, heaven had been continuously ringing with the voices of ten thousand times ten thousand angels. We've had hymn after hymn, song after song. Heaven and earth have vibrated with rafter-rousing praise. But suddenly every voice was silent and every instrument was stilled, and for half an hour no one made a sound, awaiting the next series of seven judgments—the seven trumpets.

When I read this, I think of what the prophet Habakkuk wrote: "The LORD is in his holy temple; let all the earth be silent before him" (Habakkuk 2:20). And Zechariah 2:13: "Be still before the LORD, all mankind, because he has roused himself from his holy dwelling."

Revelation 8 continues:

*And I saw seven angels who stand before God, and seven trumpets were given to them. Another angel, who had a golden censer, came and stood at the altar. He was given much incense to offer, with the prayers of all God's people, on the golden altar in front of the throne. The smoke of the incense, together with the prayers of God's people, went up before God from the angel's hand. Then the angel took the censer, filled it with fire from the altar, and hurled it on the earth; and there came peals of thunder, rumblings, flashes of lightning and an earthquake.* (vv. 2–5)

This may be the most dramatic picture of answered prayer in the Bible. A censer is a container for incense, and this one is pure gold. Perhaps it was on a golden chain. You may have seen priests perform religious rituals using these, when they've swung golden censers of incense.

The angel filled this censer with incense, which, in the Bible, is a symbol of prayer. Incense is mentioned nearly 150 times in Scripture. It is first introduced in Exodus 25, in the building of the tabernacle. The Israelites were to bring offerings for the tabernacle, including "fragrant incense" (v. 6). In Exodus 30, God gave Moses the design for the altar of incense. Verses 7–8 say, "Aaron must burn fragrant incense on the altar every morning when he tends the lamps. He must burn incense again when he lights the lamps at twilight so incense will burn regularly before the LORD for the generations to come."

The recipe for the holy incense is given in Exodus 30:34–36. According to Psalm 141:2, this burning of the holy incense at the altar of incense is a picture of our prayers: "May my prayer be set before you like incense; may the lifting up of my hands be like the evening sacrifice."

For thousands of years, Christians have prayed to God, offering their petitions, asking for things to become as they should be. They have prayed, "Thy kingdom come, Thy will be done in earth, as it is in heaven" (Matthew 6:10 KJV). They have prayed, *Even so, come, Lord Jesus* (Revelation 22:20 KJV). They have prayed, *Maranatha!*—which means, *Come, Lord!*[19]

Now these billions of prayers are about to be answered. None were unheard or forgotten. The Lord hears every syllable, every gasp and groan, every prayer that's thought or spoken or sung or written. He hears all the prayers of those who come to the throne of grace in Jesus' name. He hears your prayers. He has never forgotten a single prayer you've ever whispered to Him.

> *The Lord hears every syllable, every gasp and groan, every prayer that's thought or spoken or sung or written. He hears all the prayers of those who come to the throne of grace in Jesus' name. He hears your prayers.*

The prayers of all the ages arrived in heaven, and the angel took the prayers, filled them with fire, then threw them back to the earth, unleashing the next wave of seven disasters—the seven trumpets—which would unfold and lead up to the great tribulation.

God's kingdom is about to come, and His will is about to be done on earth as it is in heaven.

Without being emphatic, I assume that at this point we're about two to three years into the seven years predicted in Daniel 9:27. The next wave of disasters is marked by the blowing of the seven trumpets. The seven trumpet judgments remind us very much of the plagues of Egypt in Exodus 7–12. Later we'll see that the bowl judgments of Revelation 16 will do the same. In the light of Revelation's contents, we can look back at the story in Exodus 7–12 and infer that the plagues of Egypt were precursors of the events of the tribulation.

In other words, if you want to visualize a preview of the tribulation, read Exodus 7–12, which describes the judgments God spewed on Pharaoh and on the land of Egypt. Though Egypt was considered the greatest empire on earth in its day, it was reduced to tatters. When its army tried to destroy the Israelites at the Red Sea, God intervened and decimated the troops. All of this was a pale preview of the events of the tribulation.

The trumpet disasters are so severe that some interpreters place them in the second half of the seven-year period of tribulation.[20] That may be, but in keeping with a chronological approach to the book, I believe they will unfold during the last months of the first half of the tribulation, bringing the world to the brink. While intended to punish evil, these events are also designed to drive people to the gospel.

The seven trumpet judgments wind up the first half of the tribulation and trigger the events that will shift the focus of the world against the nation of Israel.

In Bible times, trumpets were used to signify battle, as when Joshua's forces marched around Jericho blowing their trumpets. Gideon did the same in his battle against Midian in Judges 7:19. Hosea 5:8 says, "Sound the trumpet. . . . Raise the battle cry." Jeremiah 51:27 says, "Blow the trumpet among the nations! Prepare the nations for battle."

So now we're ready to blow a trumpet against the nations, which brings us to event 13 on our list.

EVENT 13

# A Global Firestorm Erupts— Trumpet 1 (8:6–7)

The passage continues:

*The first angel sounded his trumpet, and there came hail and fire mixed with blood, and it was hurled down on the earth. A third of the earth was burned up, a third of the trees were burned up, and all the green grass was burned up. (8:7)*

When the first trumpet reverberates, a supernatural global storm descends on the planet, raining hail down from the sky like rounds from a machine gun, intermixed with lightning strikes that trigger massive fires. The Lord used this plague once before, on Egypt in Exodus 9:22–26, though the plague in that case serves only as a localized preview of the one in Revelation 8.

Whatever you believe about climate change, the plagues unleashed by the trumpet judgments will change the climate of earth and ruin the atmosphere once and for all. All over the globe, vast forest fires and grass fires will erupt, further darkening the skies and contaminating the air, causing loss of life, social upheaval, and the shedding of blood.

EVENT 14

# The Sea Is Contaminated— Trumpet 2 (8:8–9)

The next verses describe another ensuing catastrophe:

*The second angel sounded his trumpet, and something like a huge mountain, all ablaze, was thrown into the sea. A third of the sea turned into blood, a third of the living creatures in the sea died, and a third of the ships were destroyed.* (8:8–9)

From its description, this appears to be something like an asteroid that collides with earth, splashing down into the ocean somewhere, poisoning vast amounts of the world's oceanic systems.

Scientists use the term *impact events* to describe collisions between astronomical objects and the earth that could cause measurable and devastating effects. NASA is constantly scanning the skies for them. Scientists are continuously studying oncoming asteroids to determine the possibilities of planet-killing collisions during the next hundred years. For example, they had their eyes on one asteroid, Apophis (named for the Egyptian god of chaos), that they previously thought might strike the earth in the first half of this century.

I'm not at all suggesting asteroids are the fulfillment of Revelation 8:8–9. I'm only pointing out that the more we learn from astronomy and science, the more plausible the events in Revelation seem.

Some have speculated the object (*something like a huge mountain, all ablaze*) could be a massive nuclear bomb rather than an asteroid. We've seen scenes like this in movies, but this could be for real. It's also possible that this refers to angelic or supernatural beings causing mayhem on earth.

Whatever the nature of the object, this catastrophe will pollute a third of the ocean water. Imagine a third of all the seas and oceans in the world being contaminated and becoming rust-red like blood, which is another image from the story of the exodus.

EVENT 15

# Fresh Water Is Contaminated— Trumpet 3 (8:10–11)

The third trumpet sounds in Revelation 8:10–11, and it's hard to calculate the cataclysmic distress contained in these two verses:

> *The third angel sounded his trumpet, and a great star, blazing like a torch, fell from the sky on a third of the rivers and on the springs of water—the name of the star is Wormwood. A third of the waters turned bitter, and many people died from the waters that had become bitter.*

Again, this could be an asteroid, a meteor shower, nuclear or biological weapons, or a supernatural weapon wielded by angelic forces. Something will strike the earth, causing major failures in water supply systems around the globe.

One scientific organization announced, "It's 100 percent certain we'll be hit [by a devastating asteroid], but we're not 100 percent certain when."[21] At the same time, Stephen Hawking wrote in his final book that, in his opinion, an asteroid collision is the biggest threat to the planet.[22]

Whatever the nature of the object, it has a name: Wormwood. The Greek term used here is *Apsinthos*, which refers to a plant very bitter to the taste.[23] This plague will turn a third of the water of the earth bitter.

EVENT 16

# Sunlight Is Diminished— Trumpet 4 (8:12)

When the fourth trumpet sounds, it signals a devastating loss of sunlight.

> *The fourth angel sounded his trumpet, and a third of the sun was struck, a third of the moon, and a third of the stars, so that a third of them turned dark. A third of the day was without light, and also a third of the night.* (8:12)

This seems to refer to the amount of light reaching the earth. If the sun literally lost a third of its heat and light, life on earth would end in less than ten minutes. It takes sunlight and its heat eight minutes and twenty seconds to reach our planet.[24] But it's very plausible to envision sunlight, moonlight, and starlight being diminished by violent air pollution.

I recall when Mount Saint Helens erupted. Even though I watched the news with interest, I didn't truly understand the disaster until years later when I stood atop Seattle's Space Needle looking at the distant mountains. I saw the gap in the mountain range where the peak of Mount Saint Helens once stood. It reminded me of a first grader with missing front teeth.

The eruption of this one volcano in the spring of 1980 sent a plume of ash into the air that turned day to night in much of the Pacific Northwest. Imagine what would happen if one of earth's supervolcanoes—like the Yellowstone volcanic system—erupted. Scientists say ash would fill and filter through the sky, covering most of the continental United States. Along with the ash would come belching plumes of gases, including sulfur dioxide, causing the skies to melt in acid rain.[25]

Let me stress again, I'm not claiming these trumpet judgments necessarily involve asteroids, atomic weapons, nuclear winter, acid rain, or erupting volcanic systems. The fourth trumpet infers some kind of cataclysmic event that will make earth a much darker place. In the light of current science, technology, and issues associated with climate change, these judgments are credible and conceivable—now more than ever.

EVENT 17

# Demons Are Released to Terrorize the Earth for Five Months—Trumpet 5 (8:13–9:12)

As horrible as these things are, nothing could prepare the world for what comes next. Before the fifth trumpet, there is a special announcement from heaven:

*As I watched, I heard an eagle that was flying in midair call out in a loud voice: "Woe! Woe! Woe to the inhabitants of the earth, because of the trumpet blasts about to be sounded by the other three angels!"* (8:13)

The severity of the last three trumpet judgments warranted a special announcement about them, delivered by an eagle flying through the sky. This might be a cherub, for some cherubim are described as having eagle-like faces in Ezekiel 1:10 and Revelation 4:7. The threefold "Woe" tells us that the tribulation is about to enter a new phase in which overt warfare will spill over from the invisible realm into the visible world with massive squadrons of malevolent demonic forces.

The traumatized survivors of these first three years of great global tribulation must now brace themselves for the final six months of terrible suffering before arriving at the midpoint of the seven years. The next two trumpets involve the unleashing of the most heinous demonic forces imaginable.

Revelation 9 begins,

*The fifth angel sounded his trumpet, and I saw a star that had fallen from the sky to the earth. The star was given the key to the shaft of the Abyss.* (v. 1)

What—or who—is this star? We perhaps see him again in Revelation 20:1, which says, *And I saw an angel coming down out of heaven, having the key to the Abyss.* This may be an angel of judgment who has the key to the Abyss. In chapter 9, his job is to release the inhabitants, and in chapter 20 it's to throw Satan into the Abyss.

What, then, is the Abyss?

In simple terms, it's a supermax prison where the most malicious and malevolent demons are incarcerated. In Revelation 20:7, it is referred to as Satan's "prison." The apocryphal book of 1 Enoch (which the epistle of Jude quoted and John would have known) describes the Abyss as "the prison house of angels."[26]

At some point in the past, the archangel Lucifer led a third of the angels in rebellion against God, an event alluded to, as we'll see, in Revelation 12:4. Some of these demons are at large now, and we read about their activity throughout the Old and New Testaments. Even today, I believe demonic forces have more to do with our global conflicts than we know. But apparently some of the most brutal and heinous of the demons are incarcerated in a supernatural prison known as the Abyss.

These fallen angels are powerful in rank, and they are vicious and threatening to all God's creation. The Lord imprisoned them in a dungeon from which they could not escape—a place feared by all demonic forces. It's called the Abyss, from a Greek word meaning "a deep hole or a vast chasm."[27] It reminds me of the molten core of the earth.

In Luke 8:31, when Jesus cast a legion of demons out of a man in the region of the Gerasenes, the demons "begged Jesus repeatedly not to order them to go into the Abyss." The demons would rather inhabit a herd of swine than be sentenced to the Abyss.

The first half of Revelation 9 tells us that something or someone like a falling star will descend to the shaft of the Abyss and unlock it. Verse 2 says,

*When he opened the Abyss, smoke rose from it like the smoke from a gigantic furnace. The sun and sky were darkened by the smoke from the Abyss.*

In my mind's eye, I visualize this as a great volcano that begins spewing out not only lava, ash, gases, and smoke but frightening hordes of demonic forces. Verses 3–4 describe this as a locust invasion, but instead of harming vegetation, these locusts have a sadistic desire to sting and torture humans.

Verses 3–6 say,

*And out of the smoke locusts came down on the earth and were given power like that of scorpions. . . . They were told not to harm the grass of the earth or any plant or tree, but only those people who did not have the seal of God on their foreheads. They were not allowed to kill them but only to torture them for five months. And the agony they suffered was like that of the sting of a scorpion when it strikes. During those days people will seek death but will not find it.*

In keeping with my general approach to Revelation, I take all this with a certain literalness. These demons appear in the form of small horses with human faces and stingers in their tails (v. 7). They find pleasure in attacking and tormenting people.

I've never been stung by a scorpion, but I've read it's extremely painful. A combined team of researchers from the United States and China conducted research to explain the intensity of pain inflicted by a scorpion. Scorpions have stingers on the ends of their tails that pierce the skin and inject a particular venom that contains one hundred toxins, some of which chemically cause pain to be magnified in the way it sends signals to the brain.[28]

These painful creatures in Revelation are called "locusts," which reminds us of the book of Joel, who preached during an actual locust invasion in Old Testament days. In his first chapter, Joel described the invasion as something never before seen on this scale. "Has anything like this ever happened?" (Joel 1:2).

Later, Joel used the locust invasion to teach about the last days, and his language previewed Revelation 9:

Blow the trumpet in Zion. . . . It is close at hand—a day of darkness and gloom, a day of clouds and blackness. . . . "And afterward . . . I will show wonders in the heavens and on the earth, blood and fire and billows of smoke. The sun will be turned to darkness and the moon to blood before the coming of the great and dreadful day of the LORD. And everyone who calls on the name of the LORD will be saved." (Joel 2:1, 2, 28, 30–32)

As these things unfold in Revelation, we're not looking at actual scorpions; they are vicious demons who will torment all who haven't received Christ as Savior. It serves the purpose of judging evil, but it's also a warning that the opportunity of coming to Christ is closing.

Verse 11 describes the commander of this army of scorpion-like demons:

*They had as king over them the angel of the Abyss, whose name in Hebrew is Abaddon and in Greek is Apollyon (that is, Destroyer).*

This likely refers to Satan himself. Notice the five descriptive phrases about him.

- *king over them* [the demons]
- *angel of the Abyss*
- *Abaddon* (an Old Testament term meaning "destruction")
- *Apollyon* (the Greek equivalent of Abaddon, also meaning "destruction")
- *Destroyer* (the opposite of *Savior*)

EVENT 18

# High-Ranking Demons Are Released to Destroy a Third of Surviving Humanity—Trumpet 6 (9:13–21)

As if the scorpion-demons weren't bad enough, we're told the next two woes are even worse. The sixth trumpet sounds, and more demons are released. These are deadly. Four brutal high-ranking demonic personalities will be released with millions of killer soldiers. Revelation 9:13–16 says,

*The sixth angel sounded his trumpet, and I heard a voice. . . . It said . . . , "Release the four angels who are bound at the great river Euphrates." And the four angels who had been kept ready for this very hour and day and month and year were released to kill a third of mankind. The number of the mounted troops was twice ten thousand times ten thousand. I heard their number.*

This location seems to refer to another maximum-security prison in the spiritual realm, perhaps located in an invisible realm in Iraq (ancient Babylon) beneath the Euphrates River and near where the garden of Eden once existed.[29] This is a fascinating location because the original homeland for Abraham and the Jewish people had been beyond the Euphrates, in Ur, which was characterized by idolatry. And the Euphrates itself was ideally to be the God-established border of Israel (Joshua 1:4). The land beyond the Euphrates became the center of governments opposing Israel, such as Assyria, Babylon, and Persia. Today this area includes nations like Iraq (think of Babylon) and Iran (think of Persia).

So somewhere near the Euphrates, four demonic commanders are waiting to be released at just the appointed year, month, day, and hour. They will invade the earth and, along with two hundred million troops, bring about the death of a third of earth's remaining population. These troops are described not as locusts but as diabolical horses (Revelation 13:17).

Are the two hundred million troops human armies or demonic forces? Commentators disagree about that. As we've seen and will see again, the great military forces of the nations are mobilized and active during this time, but because Revelation 9 presents two invasions led by demons with an army of locusts and then an army of horses, I'm prone to believe both occurrences describe demonic invasions.

Michael Heiser said, "Essentially what you have described here is the prison emptied. . . . The final conflict is going to be a war between all of the supernatural forces of evil (and those humans

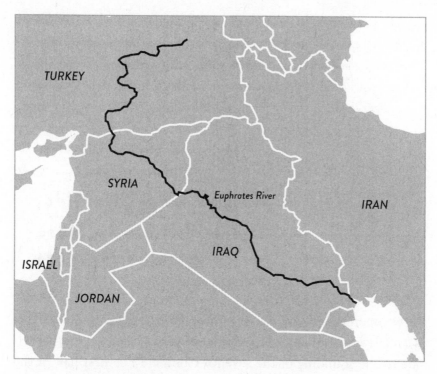

that are loyal to them) against God. Against Jesus. . . . It's cosmic evil. It's chaos. So while it's clear that the hordes here are demonic, that conclusion should not be used to eliminate the possibility of human armies . . . you've really got both going on."[30]

Revelation 9:18 says,

> *A third of mankind was killed by the three plagues of fire, smoke and sulfur that came out of their mouths.*

Earlier we saw that in Revelation 6:7–8, a fourth of humanity perished. Now a third of the remaining inhabitants of earth die. These two judgments alone have taken the lives of half the population of the world.

In spite of these horrific terrors, the surviving humans have become hardened, and most of them refuse to repent. Verses 20–21 end the chapter by saying,

*The rest of mankind who were not killed by these plagues still did not repent of the work of their hands; they did not stop worshiping demons, and idols of gold, silver, bronze, stone and wood. . . . Nor did they repent of their murders, their magic arts, their sexual immorality or their thefts.*

EVENT 19

# A Massive Angel Heralds, "There Will Be No More Delay!" (10:1–7)

As we open Revelation 10, we come to the nineteenth event. This is a relatively brief chapter (only eleven verses) that serves as a prelude to the sounding of the seventh trumpet. The first half of the tribulation is nearly over, and heaven has a dramatic announcement to make: *"There will be no more delay!"* (v. 6).

In verse 1, a mighty angel came down from heaven, *robed in a cloud, with a rainbow above his head*. His face was as bright as the sun, and his size was colossal. He planted one foot on the sea and the other on the land, and when he opened his mouth his voice reverberated through the air like thunder, like the roaring of a lion. In fact, his voice triggered a series of seven ear-shattering thunderclaps, which may represent another series of disasters, like the seven seals and the seven trumpets. John apparently understood the meaning of these seven thunderous utterances and he was about to notate them. But a voice from heaven told him, *Seal up what the seven thunders have said and do not write it down* (v. 4).

Apparently, the Lord doesn't want us to know the nature of these thunder judgments, or perhaps in His infinite mercy He will withhold them from the earth.

Verses 5–6 proceed to the main point:

*Then the angel . . . raised his right hand to heaven. And he swore by him who lives for ever and ever, who created the heavens and all that is in them, the earth and all that is in it, and the sea and all that is in it, and said, "There will be no more delay!"*

The halfway point of the tribulation is approaching, and the great tribulation is about to burst forth on the earth—the mystery of God, *just as he announced to his servants the prophets* (v. 7).

EVENT 20

# John Receives a Message About the Second Half of the Tribulation (10:8-11)

The colossal angel—some scholars believe this glorious person is Christ Himself—had another message, and this one was for John. In the angel's hand was a small scroll, and a voice from heaven told John,

*"Go, take the scroll that lies open in the hand of the angel who is standing on the sea and on the land." So I went to the angel and asked him to give me the little scroll. He said to me, "Take it and eat it. It will turn your stomach sour, but 'in your mouth it will be as sweet as honey.'"* (10:8–9)

This is exactly what happened to the prophet Ezekiel. God gave him a scroll to eat, symbolizing a warning for Israel he was to digest, internalize, and proclaim (Ezekiel 3:1–3). Because it was God's Word, it was sweet in the mouth, but because of its tone of judgment, it was hard for John to digest. We've all had the experience of eating something that tasted good, but later it didn't sit well in our stomachs. That was John's experience.

Do you remember how the first half of the tribulation opened with a scroll, which was handed to the Lamb in Revelation 5? Now the second half of the tribulation is about to open, and John saw another scroll, which he ate. It contained a warning and a message of doom for the nations that were getting ready to align against Israel and her coming Messiah. Revelation 10 ends with these words to John:

*You must prophesy again about many peoples, nations, languages and kings.* (v. 11)

It seems we are near the midpoint in the seven years of tribulation.

EVENT 21

# Two Super Prophets Are Commissioned (11:1–14)

As Revelation 11 opens, we have confirmation that the Third Temple—the Tribulation Temple—has been rebuilt on Temple Mount in Jerusalem. Apparently the Jewish state rebuilt their long-yearned-for temple during their three and a half years of relative peace while the other nations were engaged in armed conflict and dealing with the catastrophes we've already seen.

Why do I call it the Third Temple?

The first Jewish temple was built by Solomon in 2 Chronicles 3, and it was destroyed by the invading Babylonians in 587 BC in 2 Chronicles 36.

The Second Temple was built by returning Jewish exiles in Ezra

1–6 and renovated by Herod the Great in the days of Christ. Herod greatly expanded the size of the acropolis on which the temple sat, and he rebuilt it into one of the most magnificent buildings in the world. But this Second Temple was destroyed by the invading Romans in AD 70, as Jesus predicted in Matthew 24:2. If John was writing this in or around AD 95, the temple had been destroyed a quarter century before.

If you visit Jerusalem today, you'll find the Temple Mount still there occupying 36 acres (the White House sits on only 18.7 acres), dominated by two stunning Islamic structures—the Dome of the Rock and the Al-Aqsa Mosque. I've been on the Temple Mount several times and even inside the Dome of the Rock, but the politics of this site are as sensitive as a tripwire.

The western retaining wall of the Temple Mount is the holiest place on earth for religious Jewish people today because the top of the Mount itself is dominated by the Islamic structures I mentioned. One of the most moving moments in visiting Israel is joining with Jewish worshipers who are praying with their faces against the Wailing Wall.

It seems politically impossible for the Jewish people to build the Third Temple, yet there are Jewish forces preparing for it every day. The Temple Institute in Jerusalem has already prepared the sacred vessels, the priestly garments, and a model of the Holy Temple complex.[31] The cornerstone is ready and waiting, and even after two thousand years of diaspora, the dream of a Third Temple hasn't died. It's stronger than ever.

In the series of visions John had on the island of Patmos, he saw the reconstructed Third Temple and was told to measure it. Revelation 11:1–2 says,

> *I was given a reed like a measuring rod and was told, "Go and measure the temple of God and the altar, with its worshipers. But exclude the outer court; do not measure it, because it has been given to the Gentiles. They will trample the holy city for 42 months."*

In other words, the tide is about to turn against Israel. This remarkable nation, which had its beginnings with God's call of Abraham in Genesis 12, will be invaded and besieged for forty-two months—the last half of the seven years of tribulation. This will be Israel's great tribulation.

God, however, never leaves Himself without a witness. Just as He commissioned 144,000 evangelists during the first half of the tribulation, so He is about to commission two super evangelists to preach during the last half.

Revelation 11:3 says,

*I will appoint my two witnesses, and they will prophesy for 1,260 days.*

If you divide 1,260 by 30, you get 42—as in 42 months, or 3.5 years. I can't be dogmatic on the timing, but it seems to me these two prophets are commissioned now, just before the mid-point of the tribulation. I suspect their ministry will extend from just before the midpoint of the tribulation to just before the end of the seven-year period, but their ministry is described only here. Some scholars place them during the first half of the seven years of tribulation.[32] But since they are introduced here, my inclination is to view them as God's final great global evangelists who will preach in Old Jerusalem while the great tribulation is raging around them. These two evangelists will lay the foundation for the conversion of the Jewish people, which, as we'll see, will occur as Christ returns.

As the ministry of the 144,000 evangelists winds down (see event 28), the ministry of the two super evangelists begins. The gospel never ceases!

The ministry of these two super evangelists was predicted in the Old Testament book of Zechariah. In Zechariah 4, there were two men who labored mightily to lead the building of the Second Temple—Zerubbabel and Joshua. They were pictured as two olive trees providing oil for a giant lampstand.

Revelation 11:4 says of the two final witnesses,

*They are "the two olive trees" and the two lampstands, and "they stand before the Lord of the earth."*

The identities of these two men aren't given. They could be two men contemporary to the times, like the 144,000 evangelists. It isn't necessary for God to reach into biblical history to recall certain heroes. He has His people in every generation.

On the other hand, it's certainly possible these are two Old Testament heroes who God reassigns to earth for this period. Some commentators believe these two men are Moses and Elijah, the same two personalities who appeared with Jesus on the Mount of Transfiguration in Matthew 17, representing the law (Moses) and the prophets (Elijah). Certainly, these two super evangelists in Revelation 11 have the power to do miracles in the tribulation that remind us of the signs and wonders done by Moses and Elijah.

Others speculate that they are Enoch and Elijah, the only two men we know of who were transported to heaven without dying. Still others suggest the two figures are symbolic of two great groups of Christ-followers at the time—Gentile Christians and Jewish Christians. The truth is, the Lord doesn't tell us who they are, but He tells us what they do.

The passage continues:

*If anyone tries to harm them, fire comes from their mouths and devours their enemies. This is how anyone who wants to harm them must die. They have power to shut up the heavens so that it will not rain during the time they are prophesying; and they have power to turn the waters into blood and to strike the earth with every kind of plague as often as they want.* (vv. 5–6)

At some point near the close of the great tribulation, these two men will complete their assignment and be killed by the Antichrist, who is in for a rude awakening. As their bodies are displayed for all the world to see from a public square in Jerusalem, suddenly they will return to life and ascend to heaven.

> *Now when they have finished their testimony, the beast that comes up from the Abyss will attack them, and overpower and kill them. Their bodies will lie in the public square of the great city—which is figuratively called Sodom and Egypt—where also their Lord was crucified. For three and a half days some from every people, tribe, language and nation will gaze on their bodies and refuse them burial. The inhabitants of the earth will gloat over them and will celebrate by sending each other gifts, because these two prophets had tormented those who live on the earth.*
>
> *But after three and a half days the breath of life from God entered them, and they stood on their feet, and terror struck those who saw them. Then they heard a loud voice from heaven saying to them, "Come up here." And they went up to heaven in a cloud, while their enemies looked on.* (vv. 7–12)

This is one of the most dramatic moments in the great tribulation, and it coincides with a massive earthquake that will hit Jerusalem. We're told that just before and during the return of Christ, a series of earthquakes will cause the globe to shudder from pole to pole (Isaiah 29:6; Zechariah 14:4; Revelation 16:18). Verse 13 says,

> *At that very hour there was a severe earthquake and a tenth of the city collapsed. Seven thousand people were killed in the earthquake, and the survivors were terrified and gave glory to the God of heaven.*

It seems, then, that by the end of the great tribulation, there are still a few people willing to come to Christ. Indeed, as I said, the entire nation of Israel will turn to Jesus Christ just as He returns for them. Throughout these seven years, we have indications of people turning to Him, though the greatest revivals seem to occur in the earlier days, months, and years of this time of distress. But, as I'll explain later, there may well be tribulation believers on earth who escape the Antichrist's dragnets.

During most of the tribulation, Israel will be a political force in the world but not a spiritual force. The nation itself—and its capital of Jerusalem—will be a place of unrestrained sinfulness like that of Sodom in the days of Lot and of Egypt in the time of Moses. The constant preaching of these two super prophets will grate on the nerves of everyone, Jewish people and Gentiles alike, as people continue to resist the message of repentance.

Without making light of it, these two individuals seem to be the closest example in the Bible of "superheroes." They are practically invincible, and they have supernatural powers. They proclaim the gospel from the heart of Jerusalem, which agitates the powers that be. When they're finally killed, their bodies are viewed around the world, perhaps by television. To the horror of the Antichrist, they will suddenly rise to life and ascend to heaven at a moment, I believe, that closely approximates the return of Christ at the end of the seven years of tribulation.

EVENT 22

# Heaven Declares: "The Time Has Come!"—Trumpet 7 (11:15–19)

In the middle of Revelation 11, the scene shifts back to the throne room of heaven again, where worship and celebrations are continuously occurring. The first half of the tribulation began with a service of heavenly worship and courtroom drama in Revelation 4–5, and it ends with one in Revelation 11.

The contrast between the tribulation on earth and the celebration in heaven is stunning. From the worshipers in heaven comes a declaration that heaven's purposes are solidifying and prevailing.

*The seventh angel sounded his trumpet, and there were loud voices in heaven, which said, "The kingdom of the world has become the kingdom of our Lord and of his Messiah, and he will reign for ever and ever."*

*And the twenty-four elders, who were seated on their thrones before God, fell on their faces and worshiped God, saying: "We give thanks to you, Lord God Almighty, the One who is and who was, because you have taken your great power and have begun to reign. The nations were angry, and your wrath has come. The time has come."* (11:15–18)

I take this as a sign of transition from the first half of the tribulation to the last half—to the great tribulation, the time of God's wrath. In the divine courtroom, the angelic beings rejoice that the final phase of Christ's victory is about to be implemented—one that will lead directly to His return to planet earth and to the destruction of His enemies.

One final thing about Revelation 11. This chapter begins with a tour of the earthly temple and it ends with a glimpse of the heavenly temple. John was given a glimpse of the heavenly holy of holies (which was the pattern for the earthly tabernacle and temple) and of the ark of the covenant to remind him of God's faithful commitment to His special people, the Jewish people.

Verse 19 says,

*Then God's temple in heaven was opened, and within his temple was seen the ark of the covenant. And there came flashes of lightning, rumblings, peals of thunder, an earthquake and a severe hailstorm.*

The righteous and just wrath of God is reaching its point of revelation and release. This dramatic scene seems to bring the first half of the tribulation to a close, the first three and a half years.

Chapters 12–13 introduce us to the middle of the tribulation, to the false trinity, to the eruption of cosmic conflict in the physical and spiritual spheres, and to the single most defining event of the great tribulation—the setting up of the abomination of desolation in the Third Temple in Jerusalem.

Stay tuned!

# Revelation

| | Prologue 1a | Opening Vision 1b | | Mini-epistles to 7 Churches | Key Verse |
|---|---|---|---|---|---|
| CHAPTER 1<br>What you have seen… | Title, Purpose, Transmission (1–2)<br>Blessing (3)<br>Greetings (4–5a)<br>Doxology (5b–6)<br>Hymn (7)<br>Statement of Authenticity (8) | Setting (9–10)<br>Trumpet Voice (11)<br>The Glorified Christ (12–16)<br>John's Reaction (17–18)<br>Outline of Book (19)<br>Interpretation of Symbols (20) | CHAPTERS 2–3<br>What is now… | Ephesus<br>Smyrna<br>Pergamum<br>Thyatira<br>Sardis<br>Philadelphia<br>Laodicea | *The revelation from Jesus Christ, which God gave Him to show His servants what must soon take place.*<br><br>Revelation 1:1 |

| | | The Scene in Heaven | The Great Tribulation | | Return | Eternity |
|---|---|---|---|---|---|---|
| CHAPTERS 4–22<br>What you have seen… | Rapture? | God the Father<br>Holy Spirit<br>24 Elders<br>4 Creatures<br>God the Son<br>Worship<br>Scroll | Seven Seals (6–7)<br>• 2 Groups (7)<br>  • 144,000 Evangelists on Earth (7)<br>  • Tribulation Martyrs in Heaven (7)<br>Seven Trumpets (8–11)<br>• 2 Witnesses (11)<br>• Evil Trinity (12–14)<br>Seven Bowls of Wrath (15–16)<br>• World War (16)<br>  • Armageddon (16)<br>  • The Fall of Babylon (17–18) | Second Coming | Millennium & Judgment | The New Heaven & New Earth |
| 4:1 | Ch. 4–5 | | Ch. 6–18 | | Ch. 19–20 | Ch. 21–22 |

# The Midway Point of
# the Tribulation
## *Revelation 12–13*

The description of the second half of the tribulation (the three and a half years of "great tribulation") begins in Revelation 12–13 with background information to help us understand the nature of Satan's designs and the cosmic struggle now reaching its zenith. The first part of this section gives the backstory; John wanted his readers to understand the coming dramatic events within the context of the epic battle of the ages.

Revelation 12 is all about Satan and the reason for his ferocious anger against God and against Israel.

Revelation 13 describes two other evil actors—the Antichrist and the False Prophet. I believe the Antichrist is the world ruler bent on conquest who was riding the white horse in Revelation 6. Now that he has achieved a dictatorial power over the earth, he is going to be possessed by the devil, who will turn him into the most vicious human being who has ever lived.

An evil aide comes along too—the False Prophet, who is described in the last half of Revelation 13 as the beast out of the earth.

This is the anti-trinity: Satan is a kind of anti-Father, the Antichrist is diametrically opposed to Jesus Christ, and the False Prophet serves as a distortion of the Holy Spirit. Satan's desire to be like God Himself will take a horrendous turn.

In the last portion of chapter 13, the Antichrist and False Prophet will set up the abomination that causes desolation in the Third Temple. According to what Jesus predicted in Matthew 24, this is the moment when the great tribulation will begin—the last three and a half years of earth's travail.

I believe that Revelation 12–13 describes the events in the middle of the seven years of tribulation.

## The Tribulation

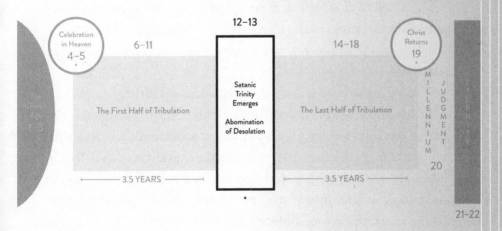

# Satan Is Expelled from Heaven and Attacks Earth with Vengeance (12:1–17)

Revelation 12 explains so much. It describes the cosmic spiritual conflict of the ages and gives us the background for how we got to this point. This chapter can be overwhelming, but I think we can demystify it by analyzing it carefully but simply. As I said earlier, we should take the Bible literally whenever possible, but much of Revelation is presented as symbols, which stand for literal items. These figures of speech are often clearly defined for us, as we'll see.

Verses 1–2 describe the historic nation of Israel as a woman, whose chosen descendants of Abraham God has set apart to provide a program of redemption for the earth:

*A great sign appeared in heaven: a woman clothed with the sun, with the moon under her feet and a crown of twelve stars on her head. She was pregnant and cried out in pain as she was about to give birth.*

The sun and moon speak of her splendor as God's chosen nation; the twelve stars point to the twelve tribes that composed the nation. This description of the woman is reminiscent of Joseph's vision in Genesis 37.

The baby she bore was the Messiah—Jesus Christ.

In his gospel—the fourth book of the New Testament—the apostle John did not give us a nativity story. He didn't deal with the events in Bethlehem the way Matthew and Luke did. But in writing Revelation, John added that information in his own unique way, telling us that in addition to the holy family, the shepherds, and the magi, there was someone else on the scene. The devil was there, too, determined to kill the child.

This evil personage called Satan was originally an archangel who mounted a rebellion against God and led a third of the angelic hosts in an insurrection. That's the essence of verses 3–4:

*Then another sign appeared in heaven: an enormous red dragon with seven heads and ten horns and seven crowns on its heads. Its tail swept a third of the stars out of the sky and flung them to the earth. The dragon stood in front of the woman who was about to give birth, so that it might devour her child the moment he was born.*

This dragon is Satan, as we see in verse 9. He tried to kill the Messiah from the very beginning of Christ's life. Remember how Herod the Great sought to destroy the Christ Child, forcing Joseph and Mary to flee to Egypt? Later, on Good Friday, Satan thought he had finally succeeded in halting God's plan of redemption by slaying Jesus on the cross.

Verse 5 is a one-verse summary of the earthly ministry of Christ.

*She gave birth to a son, a male child, who "will rule all the nations with an iron scepter." And her child was snatched up to God and to his throne.*

He was born as Israel's Messiah, lived, died, rose again, and ascended back to heaven in victory to resume His place on God's throne.

That didn't stop the devil's attacks on Israel. Just as the nation of Israel was instrumental in the Lord's first coming to earth, so His return will be within the context of unfolding Jewish drama in the last days.

That brings us to verse 6, which jumps back to the midpoint of the tribulation and says that in those desperate days, a portion of the Jewish people will flee to a place of safety where they'll weather the great tribulation:

*The woman fled into the wilderness to a place prepared for her by
God, where she might be taken care of for 1,260 days.*

In other words, in the past the nation of Israel produced the
Messiah, who the devil tried to destroy at His first coming. Now as
the great tribulation begins, the devil is still coming after the nation
of Israel, seeking to disrupt Christ's second coming. But God has
prepared a place where a remnant of Jewish people will be pro-
tected during these 1,260 days of great tribulation.

Where is this place?

I have a theory that it's modern-day Jordan, perhaps southern
Jordan in the region of the incredible hidden city of Petra, a site
I've visited twice in my life. My theory is based on Daniel 11:41,
which says, "He [the Antichrist] will invade the Beautiful Land
[Israel]. Many countries will fall, but Edom, Moab and the leaders
of Ammon will be delivered from his hand."

The lands of Edom, Moab, and Ammon represent the modern
nation of Jordan, which signed a peace treaty with Israel in 1994.
Even today, the tiny nation of Jordan buffers Israel from its more
aggressive neighbors to the east, like Syria and Iran.

The last time I was in Jordan, I traveled from Amman to Petra,
and the route took me through the ancient lands of Ammon, Moab,
and Edom. We drove on the eastern bank of the Jordan River and
stopped long enough to climb to the top of Mount Nebo, where
Moses looked out over the promised land. We passed the ruins of
Machaerus, where John the Baptist was beheaded. We saw the area
where Jesus was baptized in the Jordan. And we made our way on
down to Petra. In John's day, Petra was a teeming city, the capital
of the Nabataean Kingdom; now it's a UNESCO World Heritage
Site. We hiked down the gorge, through the narrow canyons, and
through a narrow crevice into the ruins of this rose-red city carved
into the rocks.

Could it be that somewhere in this dramatic and bleak band

of biblical geography there will be an ultimate hiding place for a portion of Jewish people during the great tribulation?

God has a plan to redeem the world. It began in Genesis 12, when He called Abraham and set him apart as the channel through whom all the world would be blessed. In accordance with God's promises in Genesis 12 and 15, Abraham's descendants became a mighty nation, and from this nation came the Messiah, whom Satan tried to destroy. The Lord Jesus, however, after finishing His redemptive work, was caught back up to heaven.

Satan, in his wrath, has sought to destroy Israel ever since, and his culminating attempt will be during the great tribulation. Perhaps he thinks by doing so he can prevent Christ's return and rob

God of His cherished and chosen people. But a remnant of Jewish people will escape from the besieged Jerusalem and be hidden for those terrible three and a half years of Jacob's distress. (Jacob was the patriarch to whom God gave the name Israel, so his descendants are the people of Israel. In Jeremiah 30:7 the tribulation is called "the time of Jacob's distress" [NASB].)

Jesus borrowed from some of the images from Jeremiah 30 when He said in Matthew 24:15–21,

> So when you see standing in the holy place "the abomination that causes desolation," spoken of through the prophet Daniel—let the reader understand—then let those who are in Judea flee to the mountains. Let no one on the housetop go down to take anything out of the house. Let no one in the field go back to get their cloak. How dreadful it will be in those days for pregnant women and nursing mothers! Pray that your flight will not take place in winter or on the Sabbath. For then there will be great distress, unequaled from the beginning of the world until now—and never to be equaled again.

A remnant of Jewish people will heed that advice and flee the city to hide in the mountains, perhaps, as I said, to a prepared place in rocky Jordan as they see the tide of events turn against them.

As that is happening on earth, something dramatic is happening in heaven. Total conflict will break out among the angelic forces of good and evil, and the devil will once and for all be expelled from access to the heavenly realms.

Revelation 12:7–9 says,

> *Then war broke out in heaven. Michael and his angels fought against the dragon, and the dragon and his angels fought back. But he was not strong enough, and they lost their place in heaven. The great dragon was hurled down—that ancient serpent called the devil, or Satan,*

*who leads the whole world astray. He was hurled to the earth, and
his angels with him.*

Three chapters in the Bible give us hints about the origin of
Satan—Isaiah 14, Ezekiel 28, and Revelation 12. Putting these
chapters together, we can reconstruct a reasonable profile of Satan's
history. He was a powerful supernatural figure who rebelled against
God when "wickedness was found" in him (Ezekiel 28:15). He led
a rebellion among the hosts of heaven and a third of God's angels
followed him (Revelation 12:4).[1] His goal became the destruction
of the Redeemer and of His channel of redemption, Israel.

For reasons we can't understand, it appears that even after their
rebellion against God at the beginning of history, Satan and his spirits still have had some access to God. They come and appear before
His throne, make accusations against believers, and make their
pleas—like diplomats from a hostile nation who can still appear
before an opposing head of state to negotiate. Remember how Satan
appeared before God in Job 1:6–7 to accuse Job and to seek his
destruction (see also 1 Kings 22:19–23 and Zechariah 3:1)? Some
people call this the divine council—supernatural personages in the
unseen realm, good and evil, who still have places of authority for
now. They still have access into God's presence.

Think of it like this. When Japanese forces attacked Pearl Harbor
in 1941 and America declared war against Japan and Germany,
hundreds of Japanese, German, and Italian diplomats were still
in the United States, and they remained here for some time. The
United States was obligated to protect these diplomats and their
families. The US State Department leased several of the nation's
finest resorts, including the Greenbrier in West Virginia and the
Grove Park Inn in Asheville, to house these diplomats.[2]

The Japanese ambassador to the United States was not expelled
until August 20, 1942. During the Cold War—even during the
Cuban Missile Crisis—Soviet diplomats remained in Washington,

DC. In modern diplomacy, when diplomats are expelled from a country, it's customary to give them seventy-two hours to depart. Expelling diplomats is a sign of imminent conflict.[3]

Like diplomats of a hostile nation, the devil and his hosts currently have some access to the heavenly realms. Satan, a brilliant archangel, can still appear before God. But at this point in Revelation 12, midway through the tribulation, the angelic warfare becomes intense. Michael, the wondrous archangel who seems to be the angelic protector of Israel, along with his angelic troops, expels the satanic hosts from the presence of heaven. They are hurled out, and they turn their full wrath on the world, on the nation of Israel, and on those still turning to Christ on earth.

This is accompanied by an official announcement from heaven in Revelation 12:10–12:

> *Now have come the salvation and the power and the kingdom of our God, and the authority of his Messiah. For the accuser of our brothers and sisters, who accuses them before our God day and night, has been hurled down. They triumphed over him by the blood of the Lamb and by the word of their testimony; they did not love their lives so much as to shrink from death. Therefore rejoice, you heavens and you who dwell in them! But woe to the earth and the sea, because the devil has gone down to you! He is filled with fury, because he knows his time is short.*

The chapter ends with the humiliated devil landing on earth determined to destroy every last Jewish person in history and every new follower of Christ he can find. A portion of the Jewish people flees for safety. Verses 13–14 say,

> *When the dragon saw that he had been hurled to the earth, he pursued the woman who had given birth to the male child. The woman was given the two wings of a great eagle, so that she might fly to the*

*place prepared for her in the wilderness, where she would be taken*
*care of for a time, times and half a time.*

This, again, describes the flight of a remnant of the Jewish people to the place God has prepared. This is biblical language. In Exodus 19:4, the Lord told the children of Israel, whom He had just delivered from Pharaoh's enslavement, "You yourselves have seen what I did to Egypt, and how I carried you on eagles' wings and brought you to myself."

While the language in Revelation 12:14 is borrowed from Exodus 19:4, it's hard for me to read this verse without visualizing an emergency airlift of some sort. I want to be cautious about turning biblical pictures into specific contrivances, but this is just so suggestive. The fleeing Jewish people will escape using two wings and flying to a place prepared in the wilderness, where they will be secure for *a time, times and half a time.* That phrase is synonymous with three and a half years (one year, two years, and a half year).

The language here is vivid and I don't know whether to interpret it literally or symbolically, but there's no doubt about its meaning. The devil tries to stop the airlift but fails. Verses 15–16 say,

*Then from his mouth the serpent spewed water like a river, to over-*
*take the woman and sweep her away with the torrent. But the earth*
*helped the woman by opening its mouth and swallowing the river that*
*the dragon had spewed out of his mouth.*

As I imagine this, I see Satan causing a massive rainstorm of hurricane force, causing flooding and threatening the air evacuation of those fleeing Israel, but the forces of nature providentially converge to save the evacuees.

The better interpretation may be this: the river is an army of human soldiers who, just as they are closing in on the evacuees, are swallowed up by the earth the way the rebellious opponents of

Moses were swallowed up when the earth opened beneath them in Numbers 16:31–34.

I prefer this interpretation because Daniel 11:40–41 describes the Antichrist's war against Israel like this: "He will invade many countries and sweep through them like a flood. He will also invade the Beautiful Land [Israel]. Many countries will fall, but Edom, Moab and the leaders of Ammon will be delivered from his hand."

John used these same figures to describe the same events. Daniel spoke of the evil armies flooding into the Middle East to surround Israel (see also Daniel 11:10).

I believe Psalm 124 was written for these Jewish evacuees to sing on that occasion. Listen to these words and compare the figures of speech—a flood, a torrent, escaping like a bird, divine deliverance:

> If the LORD had not been on our side—let Israel say—if the LORD had not been on our side when people attacked us, they would have swallowed us alive when their anger flared against us; the flood would have engulfed us, the torrent should have swept over us, the raging waters would have swept us away.
>
> Praise be to the LORD, who has not let us be torn by their teeth.
>
> We have escaped like a bird from the fowler's snare; the snare has been broken, and we have escaped.
>
> Our help is in the name of the LORD, the Maker of heaven and earth. (vv. 1–8)

When Satan fails to stop the escaping Jewish people from leaving, he is all the more infuriated. The final verse in this dramatic chapter says,

> *Then the dragon was enraged at the woman and went off to wage war against the rest of her offspring—those who keep God's commands and hold fast their testimony about Jesus.* (Revelation 12:17)

Satan, in his fury, now focuses his wrath on the remaining Jews and especially on everyone on the planet who is turning by faith to Jesus Christ. This tells us there will still be believers alive on earth who have been saved during the tribulation and have thus far escaped martyrdom. The 144,000 are still preaching, and the two super prophets are sounding off in Jerusalem. Souls are being saved! But an enraged Satan is determined to destroy every work of God on this earth. To do that, he is ready to enlist a human ally—a man of lawlessness, supercharged with satanic power.

That brings us to chapter 13 and to the next event on our list: the appearance of the Antichrist.

EVENT 24

# The Antichrist Arises (13:1–10)

Revelation 12 focuses on Satan, who views himself as a God alternative, as the anti-Father in the false trinity he is assembling. He rebelled against God at a point in the past, sought to destroy the Messiah, was thrown out of heaven with his demonic armies, tried to destroy the fleeing Jewish evacuees, and turned his wrath on the followers of Christ—the tribulation saints.

Now chapter 13 will focus on the other two members of this diabolical trinity.

Verses 1–10 describe the anti-Son or Antichrist, and verses 11–18 describe the False Prophet, who is a type of false Holy Spirit.

Verse 1 says,

*The dragon stood on the shore of the sea. And I saw a beast coming out of the sea.*

According to Revelation 17:15, this sea represents *peoples, multitudes, nations and languages,* indicating that the devil (the dragon) is recruiting his human leader from the population of the earth. I believe this will be the world leader bent on conquest who we first met in Revelation 6:2. For the past forty-two months, this man has been consolidating his power as a global tycoon and tyrant. Now he will be transformed into a satanically possessed personage of supernatural evil—the Antichrist!

Verse 1 continues:

> *It had ten horns and seven heads, with ten crowns on its horns, and on each head a blasphemous name.*

The ten horns represent a ten-nation confederacy that will compose his kingdom (like the ten toes of the statue in Daniel 2 and the ten horns of the beast in Daniel 7). The seven heads are harder to interpret but seem to represent the perfection of evil in the successive empires of human history from a biblical perspective. I'll touch on this later, for the ten horns and seven heads are explained more fully in Revelation 17.

Verse 2 describes this beast as resembling a leopard, a bear, and a lion, which reminds us of Daniel 7, where the same beasts represented the great empires of this world. This emerging global empire of the Antichrist represents the culmination of human government.

Almost every time we encounter this figure in biblical prophecy, he is said to be blasphemous, to have a big mouth that scorns God and the things of God. Daniel said about him, "The king [the Antichrist] will do as he pleases. He will exalt and magnify himself above every god and will say unheard-of things against the God of gods. He will be successful until the time of wrath is completed, for what has been determined must take place" (Daniel 11:36).

The apostle Paul said of him, "He will oppose and will exalt himself over everything that is called God or is worshiped. . . . The coming of the lawless one will be in accordance with how Satan works. He will use all sorts of displays of power through signs and wonders that serve the lie, and all the ways that wickedness deceives those who are perishing" (2 Thessalonians 2:4–10).

## Biblical Names of the Antichrist

There are over one hundred passages of Scripture that speak of the Antichrist. He is not called by the name Antichrist in the book of Revelation. That title comes from John's earlier writing, where he said, "You have heard that the antichrist is coming, even now many antichrists have come" (1 John 2:18). He went on to speak of "the spirit of the antichrist, which you have heard is coming and even now is already in the world" (4:3). In other words, many people are opposed to Christ, and the spirit of the world is, by nature, *anti* Christ. But it will culminate one day in the ultimate Antichrist. In Revelation, he is most commonly called the Beast.

Here are some of his names and titles:

- the horn (Daniel 7:8)
- a fierce-looking king (Daniel 8:23)
- a master of intrigue (Daniel 8:23)
- the ruler who will come (Daniel 9:26)
- the worthless shepherd (Zechariah 11:17)
- a contemptible person (Daniel 11:21)
- the man doomed to destruction (2 Thessalonians 2:3)
- the man of lawlessness (2 Thessalonians 2:3)
- the lawless one (2 Thessalonians 2:8–9)
- the Antichrist (1 John 2:18)
- the beast (Revelation 13:1)

Let's continue on with the last sentence in Revelation 13:2:

*The dragon gave the beast his power and his throne and great authority.*

Just as God the Father exercises authority through God the Son, so the devil will exercise his authority on earth through the Antichrist.

And now we come to the first reference of resurrection in terms of this evil ruler. Verse 3 says,

*One of the heads of the beast seemed to have a fatal wound, but the fatal wound had been healed. The whole world was filled with wonder and followed the beast.*

To all appearances, this great world ruler who dominated the conflicts of the past forty-two months was assassinated or killed in battle. We later learn he was killed (or appeared to be killed) with a sword (Revelation 13:14). But he returned to life, stunning the population of earth. The pseudo-Christ staged a pseudoresurrection.

Verse 4 says,

*People worshiped the dragon because he had given authority to the beast, and they also worshiped the beast and asked, "Who is like the beast? Who can wage war against it?"*

As this man gains control of all the global systems (governmental, economic, religious, militaristic, technological, and communicative), his vicious mouth knows no restraint during his forty-two-month reign of terror. Verses 5–6 say,

*The beast was given a mouth to utter proud words and blasphemies and to exercise its authority for forty-two months. It opened its mouth to blaspheme God, and to slander his name and his dwelling place and those who live in heaven.*

According to verse 7, the armies of the Antichrist march into and occupy Israel and Jerusalem, breaking the peace treaty inked forty-two months before. This man will become a satanic world dictator:

> *It was given power to wage war against God's holy people and to conquer them. And it was given authority over every tribe, people, language and nation. All inhabitants of the earth will worship the beast—all whose names have not been written in the Lamb's book of life, the Lamb who was slain from the creation of the world.* (vv. 7–8)

The entire world will follow this personality of ultimate evil, all except for the resisting Jewish people and any endangered Christians who have so far avoided martyrdom. These tribulation saints must now exercise *patient endurance and faithfulness* (v. 10).

EVENT 25

# The False Trinity Forms (13:11–13)

The last half of Revelation 13 describes a third diabolical character who will arise, the final personality making up the anti-trinity. He's known as the beast out of the earth or as the False Prophet. Revelation 13:11–12 says,

> *Then I saw a second beast, coming out of the earth. It had two horns like a lamb, but it spoke like a dragon. It exercised all the authority of the first beast on its behalf, and made the earth and its inhabitants worship the first beast, whose fatal wound had been healed.*

Just as the Holy Spirit brings glory to the resurrected Christ, so the False Prophet brings glory to the "resurrected" Antichrist.

**The False Trinity of the End Times**

- The dragon, Satan, the anti-Father (Revelation 12)
- The beast out of the sea, the Antichrist (Revelation 13:1–10)
- The False Prophet, the beast out of the earth, the anti–Holy Spirit (Revelation 13:11–18)

And just as the descent of the Holy Spirit on the Day of Pentecost produced signs and wonders, including fire falling from heaven, so will be the coming of the anti-Spirit. Verse 13 says,

*And it performed great signs, even causing fire to come down from heaven to the earth in full view of the people.*

This agrees with what we read in 2 Thessalonians 2:9 about the Antichrist: "The coming of the lawless one will be in accordance with how Satan works. He will use all sorts of displays of power through signs and wonders that serve the lie."

EVENT 26

# The Abomination of Desolation Is Set Up in the Temple (13:14–15)

And now we come to the most pivotal event of the tribulation—the installing of a great image in the Third Temple in Jerusalem. Verses 14–15 say,

*It ordered them to set up an image in honor of the beast who was wounded by the sword and yet lived. The second beast was given power*

*to give breath to the image of the first beast, so that the image could speak and cause all who refused to worship the image to be killed.*

As you can see, there is satanic power at work here. But this event in the rebuilt Third Temple is described consistently in Scripture and prefigured repeatedly in history.

The Third Temple, remember, was built sometime before or at the onset of the seven-year period of tribulation. The beginning of these seven years was marked by the signing of a peace treaty between the "ruler who will come" and the nation of Israel (Daniel 9:26–27). After three and a half years, the ruler gained satanic power. Now he breaks the peace treaty, sets up his own image in the temple, and demands to be worshiped.

This event is described ten times in the Bible by five different writers—Daniel, Matthew, Mark, Paul, and John. This is such an important biblical emphasis that I want to show you these ten descriptions.

- Daniel 9:27: "He will confirm a covenant with many for one 'seven.' In the middle of the 'seven' he will put an end to sacrifice and offering. And at the temple he will set up an abomination that causes desolation, until the end that is decreed is poured out on him."
- Daniel 11:31: "His armed forces will rise up to desecrate the temple fortress and will abolish the daily sacrifice. Then they will set up the abomination that causes desolation."
- Daniel 12:11: "From the time that the daily sacrifice is abolished and the abomination that causes desolation is set up, there will be 1,290 days."
- Matthew 24:15–16: "So when you see standing in the holy place 'the abomination that causes desolation,' spoken of through the prophet Daniel—let the reader understand—then let those who are in Judea flee to the mountains."

- Mark 13:14: "When you see 'the abomination that causes desolation' standing where it does not belong—let the reader understand—then let those who are in Judea flee to the mountains."
- 2 Thessalonians 2:4: "He will oppose and will exalt himself over everything that is called God or is worshiped, so that he sets himself up in God's temple, proclaiming himself to be God."
- Revelation 13:14: "It ordered them to set up an image in honor of the beast."
- Revelation 14:9: "If anyone worships the beast and its image . . ."
- Revelation 19:20: "With these signs he had deluded those who had received the mark of the beast and worshiped its image."
- Revelation 20:4: "They had not worshiped the beast or its image."

This event is also previewed in history. In 168 BC, a brutal despot named Antiochus IV Epiphanes of Syria erected a statue of Zeus in the holy of holies in the Second Temple.[4] The next year, he ordered a pig to be offered on the temple altar. When the Jewish people resisted him, he unleashed a reign of terror against Israel, which was a foreshadowing of the great tribulation.

EVENT 27

# The Mark of the Beast Is Issued (13:16–18)

Part of the satanic strategy for the world is globalized economic centralization and control. In a passage that seems more plausible than ever, Revelation 13:16–18 tells us that the Antichrist will seek to have everyone chipped or sealed for electronic tracking and commerce. The paragraph says,

> It [the False Prophet] also forced all people, great and small, rich and poor, free and slave, to receive a mark on their right hands or on their foreheads, so that they could not buy or sell unless they had the mark, which is the name of the beast or the number of its name. This calls for wisdom. Let the person who has insight calculate the number of the beast, for it is the number of a man. That number is 666.

In other words, the False Prophet will register people as part of the Antichrist's one-world economy, with everyone having an ID that is printed, tattooed, or implanted in or on their skin. This identification will be necessary for engaging in daily commerce.

Satan wants to be 7-7-7 (the perfect trinity), but he can never be more than 6-6-6. Seven is a divine number. It is repeated constantly through the book of Revelation. Satan falls short. The Antichrist falls short. The anti-Spirit falls short. God the Father is perfect, symbolized by the number seven. Six is the number of humanity (Adam was created on the sixth day of creation).[5]

Apparently, there is some symbol or logo of this evil trinity that will be imprinted on the hands or foreheads of their followers. The tribulation saints, however, will never agree to bear this mark of the Beast.

You may know that in some places even today biometric chips embedded under the skin are replacing credit cards and keys. Some governments, like those of China and the United States, are using technology to surveil their citizens, and Big Tech and Big Commerce are likely more dangerous than we realize. The mark of the Beast makes more sense to us than to any previous generation. It doesn't take an alarmist to show how our modern technology can be turned against us when it falls into the wrong hands.

# The Last Half of
# the Tribulation
## *Revelation 14–18*

For the last forty-two months, the world reeled from a series of catastrophic events that threatened the existence of the earth. A dictator finally gained the reins of global power. For one dramatic moment, everyone thought he'd been assassinated, but he virtually rose from the dead, supercharged with satanic evil. Full of fame and fury, he ordered an image of himself to be installed in the rebuilt Jewish temple. He demanded to be worshiped, which appalled the nation of Israel, prompting large numbers of Jewish people to do what Jesus had told them. When they saw the abominable image in the temple, they began fleeing to a safer spot in the wilderness, perhaps somewhere in Jordan.

The devil tried to interrupt their flight but failed. Now the full wrath of the false trinity, full of vitriol and evil and with a thirst for blood, was determined to destroy every last Christian and every last Jewish person on the planet. They were resolved to wipe out every person of God and to make Satan and his twisted trinity the lords of the earth.

We are now in the second half of Daniel's seven years. We are in the time of Jacob's distress (Jeremiah 30:7 NASB), the great tribulation. Israel will be invaded and Jerusalem surrounded and sacked. Seven final judgments—the seven bowls of wrath—are about to be poured out on the earth, especially on the human and superhuman forces of evil and their Babylonian and Roman-like empire, which will come crashing down.

Events will move quickly now as we prepare for the devil's final assault, which will trigger the Lord's victorious return in Revelation 19.

## The Tribulation

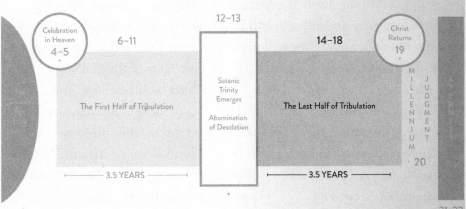

# The 144,000 Arrive
# Safely in Zion (14:1–5)

With the onset of the great tribulation, it's time to end the mission of the 144,000 and bring them home. Revelation 14 begins,

*Then I looked, and there before me was the Lamb, standing on Mount Zion, and with him 144,000 who had his name and his Father's name written on their foreheads.* (v. 1)

I believe these are the 144,000 Jewish evangelists we met in Revelation 7. Now they have completed their global mission and are gathered on Mount Zion.

There are two ways of looking at this. The location of Mount Zion could refer to Jerusalem, the capital of Israel, which, of course, is in the Middle East. If so, these 144,000 have completed their global mission and returned to Israel, where they worship and are commended. There they will minister during the chaotic remainder of the great tribulation, serving at the epicenter of the conflict.

*Throughout Revelation we see Jesus standing at the throne, indicating His work is not yet done. When a king stands, ongoing action is at hand.*

But I have a different opinion. I believe this scene is in heaven, which is referred to in the Bible as the heavenly Jerusalem, or Mount Zion (Hebrews 12:22). These heroes have now all arrived before God's throne, either by rapture or by martyrdom. Jesus is there to welcome them. After all, He has not yet arrived in earthly Jerusalem. That doesn't happen until Revelation 19. And throughout Revelation we see Jesus standing at the throne, indicating His work is not yet done. When a king stands, ongoing action is at hand.

The heavenly hosts burst into praise to welcome into heaven the 144,000 heroes, and the evangelists themselves begin to sing. They are thrilled with the success of their mission and happy to have completed their work. Verses 2–3 say,

> *And I heard a sound from heaven like the roar of rushing waters and like a loud peal of thunder. The sound I heard was like that of harpists playing their harps. And they sang a new song before the throne and before the four living creatures and the elders. No one could learn the song except the 144,000 who had been redeemed from the earth.*

We're also told that despite the temptation and evil these evangelists faced during their earthly work, not one of them had created a scandal or destroyed their mission by moral failure. Verses 4–5 say,

> *These are those who did not defile themselves with women, for they remained virgins. They follow the Lamb wherever he goes. They were purchased from among mankind and offered as firstfruits to God and the Lamb. No lie was found in their mouths; they are blameless.*

The term *firstfruits* indicates the eventual conversion of the Jewish people. These evangelists were precursors and harbingers of millions of Jewish people who will be saved just as Jesus returns to earth, as we'll see later.

# Three Angels Deliver Final Messages to the Earth (14:6–13)

Now that we're in the great tribulation, the action moves swiftly. The next event is a trio of messages from heaven to earth, delivered by angels. With the 144,000 gone and any surviving Christians in hiding and living in great danger, the Lord sends three angels to continue proclaiming the eternal gospel and warning the remaining population of earth.

To the very end, God desires for people to be redeemed by the blood of Jesus.

### The First Angel

We meet the first angelic messenger in verses 6–7:

> *Then I saw another angel flying in midair, and he had the eternal gospel to proclaim to those who live on the earth—to every nation, tribe, language and people. He said in a loud voice, "Fear God and give him glory, because the hour of his judgment has come. Worship him who made the heavens, the earth, the sea and the springs of water."*

Imagine this angel crisscrossing the globe, giving the world yet another chance to fear God and yield their lives to Jesus Christ. He is proclaiming the eternal gospel as if by a loudspeaker to the remaining inhabitants on earth.

### The Second Angel

A second angel is dispatched, and his message is a declaration of doom, warning that the kingdom of the Antichrist is about to crumble. Verse 8 says,

*A second angel followed and said, "'Fallen! Fallen is Babylon the Great,' which made all the nations drink the maddening wine of her adulteries."*

The word *fallen* is in a Greek tense indicating that while the action is not yet done, it is as good as done. Maybe you've heard someone in a television drama say, "He's a dead man," indicating the victim is about to be hunted down and killed. This is a pronouncement of doom on Babylon.

Notice the phrase *Babylon the Great.* This is the first occurrence of the word *Babylon* in the book of Revelation, but it introduces an important theme. The great tribulation empire of the Antichrist is code-named Babylon in these final chapters of Revelation. This relates to a consistent emphasis throughout Scripture.

In Genesis, we're told about a ruthless dictator named Nimrod, who became "a mighty hunter" and who founded an evil city known as Babylon (1:9–10). Shortly afterward, the inhabitants of that city tried to build a tower to rival God. From that point on throughout Scripture, Babylon (which is roughly equivalent to the area of modern-day Iraq) represented a human empire opposed to God and bent on the destruction of Israel.

Under King Nebuchadnezzar, it was the Babylonian Empire that destroyed the nation of Judah and the city of Jerusalem in 587 BC. Now in Revelation, this designation is given for the Antichrist's empire as he seeks to do the same.

Does that mean the anti-Christian empire will literally be in modern-day Iraq? Will it be centered in or near the site of ancient Babylon? Maybe, but not necessarily. The city of Babylon still existed in John's day, though without its former glory.[1]

We simply know that in God's eyes, the final global empire is a revival of the worst forms of anti-Semitic and anti-Christian evil. The book of Daniel indicates that it will also be like a revival of the Roman Empire.

The Antichrist's empire will be like Babylon in its hatred of the God of heaven and like Rome in its military brutality.

Our headlines are dominated by political forces in the areas of ancient Babylon and Persia that are intent on developing nuclear arsenals to obliterate the state of Israel. We're all aware that Israel has faced existential threats since its founding in 1948, and some of her neighbors hate her with demonic vengeance and want to wipe the Jewish state off the face of the earth.

So the capital city and empire of the Beast could have its head-quarters on or near the ancient city of Babylon, which is today in ruins. One advocate for this position, Dr. Henry Morris, said,

> Babylon is indeed a prime prospect for rebuilding, entirely apart from any prophetic intimations. Its location is the most ideal in the world for any kind of international center. Not only is it in the beautiful and fertile Tigris Euphrates plain, but it is near some of the world's richest oil reserves. . . .
>
> Babylon is very near the geographical center for all the world's land masses. It is within navigable distances of the Persian Gulf and is at the crossroads of the three great continents of Europe, Asia, and Africa.
>
> Thus there is no more ideal location anywhere for a world trade center, a world communication center, a world banking center, a world education center, or especially, a world capital![2]

On the other hand, when the Antichrist's capital city of Babylon collapses in Revelation 18:17–18, we're told sea captains and sailors will stand far off, watching the smoke rising to the sky, and saying in shock and sadness, "Was there ever a city like this great city?"

The original city of Babylon (about fifty miles south of Baghdad) is landlocked from the sea, though situated on the Euphrates River, giving it access to the Persian Gulf. It's certainly possible that the Antichrist could choose this location to build his capital and that the sailors who mourn its destruction could be plying the Euphrates or even seeing some smoke drift through the sky from three hundred miles away on the Persian Gulf.

My own opinion, based on Daniel 2 and 7, is that the Antichrist's empire will be similar to the Roman Empire in the days of Christ, a confederation of nations that stretches across Mediterranean Europe, Turkey, and the Islamic Near East, including the Persian Gulf countries, and circles around North Africa, which is currently littered with failed Islamic states and terrorist groups. The Antichrist's international friends and foes may extend northward into Russia and eastward into China, as we'll see in the book of Ezekiel.

According to Daniel 2:42–43, the Antichrist's Neo-Roman Empire will be "partly strong and partly brittle. . . . so the people will be a mixture and will not remain united." In other words, the Antichrist will struggle to hold his confederacy together, but it will be extremely brutal. Daniel described it as "terrifying and frightening and very powerful. It had large iron teeth; it crushed and devoured its victims and trampled underfoot whatever was left. It was different from all the former [empires], and it had ten horns [an alliance of ten powerful kingdoms or nations]" (Daniel 7:7).

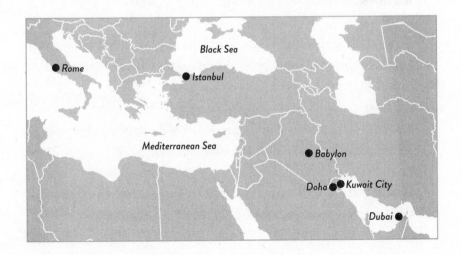

The exact location of the capital city code-named Babylon is speculation on my part, but maybe it'll prompt you to grab a map and do some study on your own. The great capital of the Antichrist— his center of government, culture, religion, and economy—could be a city on the Persian Gulf like Kuwait City, Doha, or Dubai. Or it could be a Mediterranean port like Istanbul (which sits between the Sea of Marmara and the Black Sea). Or it could be Rome or, yes, a city rebuilt on or near the ruins of ancient Babylon.

I'm unsure about the location of the Antichrist's capital city, but there's no doubt about how it will all end. The message of the second angel is, *Fallen! Fallen is Babylon the Great,* which is actually an Old Testament prophecy from Isaiah 21:9.

## The Third Angel

After the second angel completes his circuit, a third and final angel flies from heaven with a message for the entire world—a warning. Verses 9–10 say,

> *A third angel followed them and said in a loud voice: "If anyone worships the beast and its image and receives its mark on their forehead or on their hand, they, too, will drink the wine of God's fury, which has been poured full strength into the cup of his wrath."*

This message is to the entire world, but it's intended to reinforce the hearts of the remaining believers on earth, who are being hunted down and martyred. Verse 12 says,

> *This calls for patient endurance on the part of the people of God who keep his commands and remain faithful to Jesus.*

I believe there will be survivors of the great tribulation, including Christians who have escaped the wrath of the Enemy.

Yet many believers will be slain. In verse 13, we have a remarkable added affirmation from heaven, including a rare occurrence of words attributed directly to the Holy Spirit:

> *Then I heard a voice from heaven say, "Write this: Blessed are the dead who die in the Lord from now on."*
>
> *"Yes," says the Spirit, "they will rest from their labor, for their deeds will follow them."*

This verse refers especially to those who will die for Christ during the great tribulation, but what it says about death is applicable for Christians of all ages. There are three things we can learn here about dying:

- Death is actually a blessing for a follower of Christ.
- Death represents a resting from our earthly labors and concerns.
- Our works will follow us. The good we've done on earth will continue to accrue. Our influence will remain and have a pass-along, ripple effect. The full results of our lives cannot be calculated until the dawn of eternity.

EVENT 30

# Christ's Declaration of War (14:14–16)

As events begin to reach a catastrophic climax, Jesus speaks. His words are a declaration of war. In Revelation 14:14, the Lord Jesus Christ declares war on the global kingdom of the Antichrist, which is centered in "Babylon."

Verse 14 describes the Lord like this:

*I looked, and there before me was a white cloud, and seated on the cloud was one like a son of man with a crown of gold on his head and a sharp sickle in his hand.*

The Lord Jesus takes the sickle and swings it over the earth, indicating the time has now come for the harvest, the time when those who have sown evil will reap evil and be reaped. Jesus used a similar metaphor in Matthew 13:39 when He said, "The harvest is the end of the age, and the harvesters are angels."

This is a war scythe, a declaration of war. In some of the great revolutions in history, peasants and rebels used war scythes to attack those entrenched in power. Farmers who grew up working the fields skillfully mowed down weeds with their hand scythes. The same tools made deadly weapons in combat. Because of its curved blade, a scythe could be more easily drawn out of its victim. Its penetration brought painful death, but it could be extracted with the flick of a wrist and aimed at the next enemy combatant quickly.[3]

The Lord Jesus used this symbol as a declaration of war, fulfilling a remarkable prophecy made by the Old Testament prophet Joel, who said,

"Let the nations be roused; let them advance to the Valley of Jehoshaphat [Armageddon], for there I will sit to judge all the nations on every side. Swing the sickle, for the harvest is ripe. Come, trample the grapes, for the winepress is full and the vats overflow—so great is their wickedness!"

Multitudes, multitudes in the valley of decision! For the day of the LORD is near in the valley of decision. The sun and moon will be darkened, and the stars no longer shine. The LORD will roar from Zion and thunder from Jerusalem; the earth and the heavens will tremble. But the LORD will be a refuge for his people, a stronghold for the people of Israel. (3:12–16)

My guess is that we're about a year into the great tribulation, and the false trinity has been seething in anger over Israel's resistance to worshiping the idol in the temple. Battle plans have been drawn, troops moved, strategies implemented, and armies advanced to the borders of Israel as they start to occupy the promised land.

## The Seven Beatitudes of Revelation

1. *Blessed is the one who reads aloud the words of this prophecy, and blessed are those who hear it and take to heart what is written in it, because the time is near.* (1:3)
2. *"Blessed are the dead who die in the Lord from now on."* (14:13)
3. *"Blessed is the one who stays awake and remains clothed."* (16:15)
4. *"Blessed are those who are invited to the wedding supper of the Lamb!"* (19:9)
5. *Blessed and holy are those who share in the first resurrection.* (20:6)
6. *"Look, I am coming soon! Blessed is the one who keeps the words of the prophecy written in this scroll."* (22:7)
7. *"Blessed are those who wash their robes, that they may have the right to the tree of life and may go through the gates into the city."* (22:14)

In His usual bounty, God actually wove eight blessings into the seven, for the first one is repeated twice, once for those who read and once for those who hear and take the message to heart. This is the symphonic octave of Revelation—eight notes of eternal blessings.

# Warfare Erupts Around Israel (14:17–20)

The next paragraph advances the action. The image of the sickle continues, letting us know that by this point bloody warfare is taking place within the boundaries of Israel and around Jerusalem.

Because the Jewish people refused to honor the abominable image of the Antichrist in their temple, the Antichrist is determined—as so many despots were throughout history—to destroy Israel brutally and totally. As the conflict rages and armies clash, verse 20 says,

> *They were trampled in the winepress outside the city [Jerusalem], and blood flowed out of the press, rising as high as the horses' bridles for a distance of 1,600 stadia.*

Still using the language of Joel, we're told the blood spills like juice from a vineyard's grape press.

Notice that the battle is still outside of Jerusalem. Israeli defense forces are putting up a strong fight. The city of Jerusalem hasn't yet been breached, but Israel is under invasion. According to Luke 21:24, many Jewish people will be killed and others will be taken prisoner and transported to various nations.

The designated distance (1,600 stadia) equals approximately 180 miles, which means the field of battle will be within a 90-mile radius of Jerusalem.

By car, the site of Megiddo (which overlooks the valley of Armageddon) is about eighty miles from Jerusalem. As we'll see, the valley of Armageddon seems to be where the Antichrist establishes his field headquarters, but the thrust of the battle is against Jerusalem.

We're told this initial invasion of Israel will be so intense the blood will rise as high as horses' bridles. I take this to mean that in the worst war zones the blood will splatter five and six feet into the air.

I believe the warfare described in Revelation 14:20 is part of the military campaigns referred to in the book of Ezekiel as the battle of Gog and Magog. Ezekiel 38 describes the last half of the great tribulation and the looming battle of Armageddon. *Gog* is a code word for the Antichrist, and *Magog* is code for his empire.[4]

According to Ezekiel 38:8, forces from these nations will invade Israel in a coming period of time described as "after many days" and "in future years."

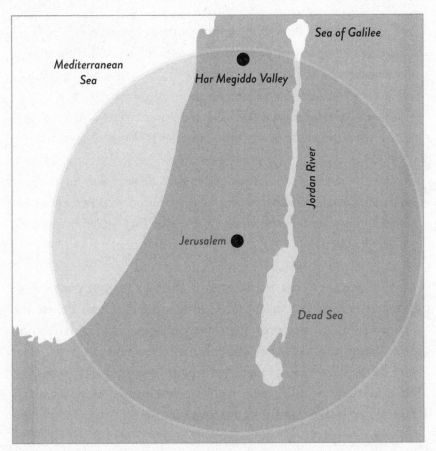

# The Seven Last Angels of the Last Plagues Appear (15:1–8)

As the armies of the world continue to aim their ships, planes, missiles, and troops toward Israel, the Lord hinders them with a final series of global disasters that bring His righteous wrath to a grand finale in human history. This brings us to the final seven disasters—the seven bowls of wrath that are poured out on the world.

Revelation 15:1 says,

> *I saw in heaven another great and marvelous sign: seven angels with the seven last plagues—last, because with them God's wrath is completed.*

The entirety of Revelation 15 is a glorious scene as heaven prepares to unleash these seven final judgments. Verse 2 says,

> *And I saw what looked like a sea of glass glowing with fire and, standing beside the sea, those who had been victorious over the beast and its image and over the number of its name. They held harps given them by God.*

As we've seen, the sea of glass is the vast crystal platform or square on which the throne of God is located. There before the throne are more martyrs—men, women, boys, and girls who, in the opening months of the great tribulation, turned to Christ. They were hunted down and killed, perhaps in ways beyond imagining. But now they are in heaven, and they've immediately formed a choir. Their hearts are full of song and praise.

Verse 3 says,

*And [they] sang the song of God's servant Moses and of the Lamb.*

The beautiful words of their song are given in verses 3–4:

*Great and marvelous are your deeds, Lord God Almighty. Just and true are your ways, King of the nations. Who will not fear you, Lord, and bring glory to your name?*

Why is this called the song of Moses and of the Lamb?

Like the trumpets, these bowls of wrath are going to hark back to the plagues Moses initiated against Egypt in the book of Exodus. The plagues of Egypt that devastated Pharaoh and saved the Jewish people were previews of these last seven bowls of wrath that will break the grip of the Antichrist and save the Jewish people.

Remember, the story of the exodus was in some sense a type of the great tribulation. What Moses did to Egypt, Jesus will do to the final evil world empire. Pharaoh, then, is another plausible biblical type of the Antichrist. He sought to enslave and annihilate the Jewish race, but God supernaturally delivered them. He tried to destroy them as they were fleeing his clutches, as the Antichrist will do.

Exodus 15 records the words sung by the multitude that had passed through parted waters of the Red Sea. Liberated and safe from the horrors of Pharaoh, they burst into spontaneous praise. In the same way, Revelation 15 records the words sung by the multitude that has come through the tribulation and is now liberated from the horrors of the Antichrist, safe on the heavenly shore. The worshipers in heaven were thinking of the first recorded biblical hymn in Exodus 15 as they sang their song of praise.

*What Moses did to Egypt, Jesus will do to the final evil world empire.*

*After this I looked, and I saw in heaven the temple—that is, the tabernacle of the covenant law—and it was opened. Out of the temple*

117

*came the seven angels with the seven plagues. They were dressed in clean, shining linen and wore golden sashes around their chests. Then one of the four living creatures gave to the seven angels seven golden bowls filled with the wrath of God, who lives for ever and ever. And the temple was filled with smoke from the glory of God and from his power, and no one could enter the temple until the seven plagues of the seven angels were completed.* (Revelation 15:5–8)

As the seven angels receive their golden bowls of wrath, the glorious cloud of God's presence fills heaven. Things are coming quickly to a dramatic zenith. From this point, the action moves swiftly—all seven bowls of wrath are poured out in Revelation 16, and all roads lead to Armageddon.

EVENT 33

# Global Contagion Spreads— Bowl 1 (16:1–2)

In Revelation 16:1, John heard a loud voice commanding the angels: *"Go, pour out the seven bowls of God's wrath on the earth."*

At this point, I want to pause to discuss the subject of God's wrath. This concept used to bother me because wrath seemed an inappropriate attitude for a perfect and eternal Being like God. But I came to realize this word does not imply anything akin to a temper tantrum or a loss of self-control. It is a proper, necessary response to the evil that causes all the suffering and misery in the world.

The presence of absolute truth and objective good demands a moral response to deception and to evil. What kind of God could look at genocide, torture, rape, and sin of any kind without responding in righteousness and holiness? The wrath of God is His proper judicial response to evil as He seeks to direct people toward repentance or (if they fail to respond to Him) to judge them for their corruption.

*The presence of absolute truth and objective good demands a moral response to deception and to evil.*

Revelation 16:2 says,

*The first angel went and poured out his bowl on the land, and ugly, festering sores broke out on the people who had the mark of the beast and worshiped its image.*

Suddenly a new pandemic sweeps over the earth, a skin contagion similar to the plague of boils that struck Egypt in Exodus 9. If you've ever had a bad case of poison ivy—I have!—multiply that by several factors. Imagine almost everyone on earth spreading this from person to person until the entire world—except for the tribulation believers—is scratching and itching and oozing. It undoubtedly slows down the military forces converging on Israel. The Lord has joined the battle on Israel's side, and the Antichrist is powerless to stop the dermatological plague.

Those whose skin was marked with the sign of the Beast are now marked with festering boils.

EVENT 34

# The Seas Are Destroyed— Bowl 2 (16:3)

The next verse says,

*The second angel poured out his bowl on the sea, and it turned into blood like that of a dead person, and every living thing in the sea died.* (16:3)

This plague, too, harks back to the book of Exodus, when Moses turned the Nile River into blood (Exodus 7). The world's oceans were already damaged by the second trumpet, but now they turn into a thick, red swamp, which undoubtedly slows down the ships and submarines heading toward the coast of Israel.

Elsewhere in Revelation, the idea of the "sea" represents the people of the earth (17:15), so some commentators think this is figurative for the suffering of humanity. But the Antichrist's world is coming to an end, and the physical realm is disintegrating into chaos. To me, this refers to the destruction of the world's oceanic systems.

Consider this. The oceans are more polluted now than at any time in history. Even as I write this, a major oil spill has ruined a section of an American coastline. Every year, 17.6 billion tons of plastic land in the ocean, and one garbage patch twice the size of Texas floats around in the Pacific. Because of toxic runoffs, scientists are finding more "dead zones" in our oceans, including one in the Gulf of Mexico nearly the size of New Jersey.[5]

Things are going to become much worse at the end of the tribulation. The entire world of our oceans will become a dead zone.

EVENT 35

# The Fresh Water Is Polluted— Bowl 3 (16:4–7)

In another blow to the world's military leaders and their converging armies, fresh drinking water becomes very hard to find. Revelation 16:4 says,

*The third angel poured out his bowl on the rivers and springs of water, and they became blood.*

That is what happened in Egypt as well. It wasn't just the Nile that turned to blood. Exodus 7:19 says Aaron lifted his staff, and the streams, canals, ponds, and reservoirs all turned to blood, even the water sitting in pitchers and vessels. The Egyptians had to dig new wells trying to find water to stave off thirst (v. 24). During the final months of the great tribulation, the entire world will face a severe shortage of drinking water.

This judgment is so severe there's a pause in the text as the angels acknowledge that the Lord does, in fact, know what He is doing and that He is acting justly and righteously and wisely (vv. 5–7).

EVENT 36

# Intense Heat Scorches the Planet—Bowl 4 (16:8–9)

The fourth bowl of wrath involves a series of flares from the sun that heat the earth like a furnace. Revelation 16:8–9 says,

*The fourth angel poured out his bowl on the sun, and the sun was allowed to scorch people with fire. They were seared by the intense heat and they cursed the name of God, who had control over these plagues, but they refused to repent and glorify him.*

This is ultimate global warming. Apparently the sun experiences solar flares and bursts of electromagnetic radiation that scorch people and perhaps also cause radio blackouts and further disruptions of technology.

All these plagues are warnings to motivate people toward repentance while time remains, but people no longer seem responsive to the gospel. The solar disruptions and intense heat, again, create problems for the military forces converging on Israel. Imagine the fury of the foul-mouthed Antichrist as he tries to cope with these cascading disasters. He is supernaturally empowered by Satan, but Satan's power has its limits.

The Old Testament ends with a reference to this particular plague. Malachi 4:1 says, "Surely the day is coming; it will burn like a furnace. All the arrogant and every evildoer will be stubble, and the day that is coming will set them on fire."

# Darkness Covers the World— Bowl 5 (16:10–11)

Like a whipsaw, the next plague is another replay of one of the Egyptian plagues—darkness. Revelation 16:10–11 says,

> *The fifth angel poured out his bowl on the throne of the beast, and its kingdom was plunged into darkness. People gnawed their tongues in agony and cursed the God of heaven because of their pains and their sores, but they refused to repent of what they had done.*

It's interesting that this judgment is directed at the throne of the Antichrist, which indicates his headquarters is targeted. It could be that the entire world is plunged into literal darkness, but what if it refers to a worldwide blackout, to the failure of the power grid and the disruption of global technology?

Whatever form it takes, the Bible repeatedly warns of a day of coming darkness and blackness. The prophet Amos wrote, "Why do you long for the day of the LORD? That day will be darkness, not light" (Amos 5:18).

Isaiah said, "The rising sun will be darkened and the moon will not give its light" (Isaiah 13:10).

Zephaniah 1:15 says, "That day will be a day of wrath—a day of distress and anguish, a day of trouble and ruin, a day of darkness and gloom, a day of clouds and blackness."

The Lord Jesus said, "But in those days, following that distress, 'the sun will be darkened, and the moon will not give its light'" (Mark 13:24).

To me, it's remarkable how the prophetic passages of the Bible seem to converge into a consistent picture of these dramatic days.

EVENT 38

# The Euphrates Dries Up—Bowl 6 (16:12)

Despite all these strategic challenges, the armies of the world are still hobbling toward Jerusalem, including vast armies from Asia, drawn there by the Antichrist and his deceptive demons. In this case, the Lord seems to help them. He wants them to gather on Israel's northern plains, where He will judge them in the valley of Armageddon.

Revelation 16:12 says,

*The sixth angel poured out his bowl on the great river Euphrates, and its water was dried up to prepare the way for the kings from the East.*

Ezekiel 38–39 indicates armies from north of Israel, from the lands of ancient Persia, and from North Africa will converge for this battle. Revelation 16:12 tells us armies from Asia will mobilize and move toward Israel. Drawing a straight eastern line from Israel takes you through Iraq, Iran, Pakistan, Afghanistan, India, and China.

The connection to China is especially intriguing. Turn on the news anytime, it seems, and you'll hear of China's aggressive drive to become the world's one and only superpower. The government's repression of its people, its surveillance of its citizens, its intrusive use of electronic monitors and autocratic spying is deeply disturbing. Its growing military force is a threat unseen in human history.[6]

According to the book of Joshua, the Euphrates River is the boundary between the Holy Land and Asia (1:4). This passage in Revelation says that the Euphrates will dry up to allow these armies to march without hindrance toward Israel. When John wrote these words, it must have seemed inconceivable. But now the nation of Turkey has built immense dams across the Euphrates, and in recent years there have been moments when the waters have been blocked and the Euphrates has gone dry. This is no longer an implausible picture.

There are two popular views about the armies coming from the East. My own view is they are part of the coalition of nations deceived by demons and marching to confront and destroy Israel. Some prophecy students believe they are coming to attack the Antichrist because he's losing his grip on power. This is why God dried the Euphrates to let them march. The basis for this interpretation is Daniel 11:41–45:

> He [the Antichrist] will also invade the Beautiful Land [Israel]. Many countries will fall, but Edom, Moab and the leaders of Ammon [the modern nation of Jordan] will be delivered from his hand. He will extend his power over many countries. . . . But reports from the east and the north will alarm him, and he will set out in a great rage to destroy and annihilate many. He will pitch his royal tents between the seas [Armageddon and the roads leading to Jerusalem are between the Mediterranean Sea, the

Sea of Galilee, and the Dead Sea] at the beautiful holy mountain [Jerusalem]. Yet he will come to his end, and no one will help him.

John MacArthur boiled it down to this:

God supernaturally will dry up [the Euphrates] to make way for the eastern confederation to reach Israel. God providentially draws these kings and their armies in order to destroy them in the battle of Armageddon. Their reason for coming may be to rebel against Antichrist, whose failure to alleviate the world's suffering will no doubt erode his popularity. Or this may be a final act of rabid anti-Semitism intent on destroying Israel, perhaps in retaliation for the plagues sent by her God.[7]

Whatever the motive, the armies from Asia, crazed by the plagues and full of fury, will march across the dry Euphrates the way the children of Israel crossed into the promised land through the parted waters of the Jordan River in the days of Joshua.

EVENT 39

# The World's Armies Converge at Armageddon (16:13–16)

As these armies pass over the Euphrates, the evil trinity seem to realize they are in an unprecedented war, facing extraordinary challenges. As we saw from Daniel 2, the Antichrist will have trouble maintaining the unity of his evil empire as he battles the supernatural plagues sent against him. Just as iron mixed with clay will not remain united, Daniel said, neither will this final world empire (Daniel 2:43). Needing additional supernatural support, the

Antichrist will summon three more malicious demons—perhaps the most powerful ever seen in the cosmos—as the troops from Asia cross the dry bed of the Euphrates River. The pseudo-trinity will release their remaining demons, who invade the world like the plague of frogs in Exodus 7–8, and deceive the kings by telling them there is still hope for a victory.

Here's how it's put in Revelation 16:13–16:

> *Then I saw three impure spirits that looked like frogs; they came out of the mouth of the dragon, out of the mouth of the beast and out of the mouth of the false prophet. They are demonic spirits that perform signs, and they go out to the kings of the whole world, to gather them for the battle on the great day of God Almighty. . . . Then they gathered the kings together to the place that in Hebrew is called Armageddon.*

I've taken many tour groups to the great valley of Armageddon, which is about ten miles from Nazareth in the Lower Galilee. Looking out over the vast plains, the scene is breathtaking. This is the breadbasket of Israel, a huge agricultural area like the San Joaquin Valley of California.

The word *armageddon* comes from the Hebrew *Har Megiddo*. The word *har* means "mountain."[8] Megiddo is the ancient name of a strategic hilltop city. From the ruins of Megiddo, it's amazing to look out over the horizon and imagine the coming day of conflict.

This has been called the world's most perfect battleground. According to historians, over thirty major military conflicts have occurred in this valley. In fact, the first recorded battle in world history was fought here—a campaign by Egyptian pharaoh Thutmose III, who wanted to expand Egypt's empire in the 1400s BC. Thutmose has been called the Napoleon of Egypt. He fought a coalition of Canaanite tribes, and the events of the battle were recorded and later found in an ancient temple in Luxor, Egypt. Thutmose's victory allowed him to continue marching into near Asia to expand his empire.[9]

How interesting that the site of the first significantly recorded battle will also become the staging area for the final battle in world history.

I suspect Armageddon will be the central military command headquarters for the Antichrist, but we know the battle itself will rage across Israel, ninety miles in all directions from Jerusalem, and at last the Holy City itself will be breached and will fall.

Some commentators translate the Hebrew word for *Armageddon* as referring to Jerusalem.[10] The city of Jerusalem is clearly the target, but the traditional understanding is that the vast plains of Armageddon—the Jezreel Valley, also called the Valley of Megiddo—will be the command post.

The most vivid description of this battle occurs in the book of Zechariah, and the information is so important I want to show it to you here. Read these words from Zechariah 12:

> A prophecy: The word of the LORD concerning Israel.
>
> The LORD, who stretches out the heavens, who lays the foundation of the earth, and who forms the human spirit within a person, declares: "I am going to make Jerusalem a cup that sends all the surrounding peoples reeling. Judah will be besieged as well as Jerusalem. On that day, when all the nations of the earth are gathered against her, I will make Jerusalem an unmovable rock for all the nations. . . . On that day, I will strike every horse with panic and its rider with madness," declares the LORD. . . .
>
> "On that day I will set out to destroy all the nations that attack Jerusalem." (vv. 1–4, 9)

More details emerge in Zechariah 14, which speaks of urban conflict and terrible military atrocities in the center of Jerusalem—"Within your very walls" (v. 1)—indicating the Ottoman-era walls of the Old City will be breached and hand-to-hand fighting will rage in the shadow of the Temple Mount. The city will fall, and half of the survivors will be herded out of the city, presumably into hastily prepared prisoner-of-war camps. But something will interrupt the process while half of the population is still in the city.

Zechariah 14:1–2 says, "A day of the LORD is coming, Jerusalem, when your possessions will be plundered and divided up within your very walls. I will gather all the nations to Jerusalem to fight against it; the city will be captured, the houses ransacked, and the women raped. Half of the city will go into exile, but the rest of the people will not be taken from the city."

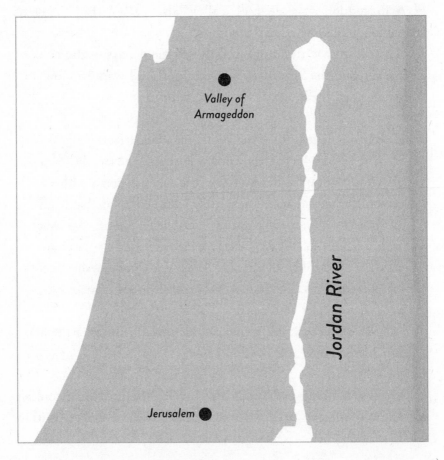

# Earthquakes and Extreme Weather Devastate What's Left of Earth—Bowl 7 (16:17-21)

What interrupts the defeat of the Jewish people in Jerusalem and keeps them from going into exile? At the very moment when the Antichrist thinks he has won the battle, a global series of earthquakes will strike the planet, ripping down cities, disrupting any remaining infrastructure, and killing millions of people. This is the seventh bowl of wrath.

*The seventh angel poured out his bowl into the air, and out of the temple came a loud voice from the throne, saying, "It is done!" Then there came flashes of lightning, rumblings, peals of thunder and a severe earthquake. No earthquake like it has ever occurred since mankind has been on earth, so tremendous was the quake. The great city split into three parts, and the cities of the nations collapsed. God remembered Babylon the Great and gave her the cup filled with the wine of the fury of his wrath. (16:17-21)*

The "great city" that split into three parts could be Jerusalem, but I take it to be Babylon. As the cities of the nation collapse, God singles out Babylon for special judgment *and gave her the cup filled with the wine of the fury of his wrath.* The city is broken into three sections—three fault lines shifting at once, causing total apocalyptic destruction. (In the next two chapters of Revelation, John is going to give us a detailed view of the fall and ruin of this great city and all its evil systems.)

This series of storms and global earthquakes will trigger massive tsunamis that will sweep over islands and cover high mountains. Verse 20 says,

*Every island fled away and the mountains could not be found.*

But that's not all. In the final outpouring of wrath on the evil of planet earth, powerful storms will blanket the globe, producing hailstones unlike anything before imagined. Verse 21 goes on to tell us,

*From the sky huge hailstones, each weighing about a hundred pounds, fell on people. And they cursed God on account of the plague of hail, because the plague was so terrible.*

This is the last of the bowls of wrath, the final series of global catastrophes that leaves the world in a smoldering, crumbling heap. As the globe's tectonic plates break apart, seismic forces convulse the world and cause the cities of the world to collapse. At the same time, a global electrical storm sweeps over the earth, and hailstones the size of boulders fall from the sky as if they were targeting people.

If you've ever seen some apocalyptic movies, you can picture skyscrapers tumbling, buildings collapsing, and storms of supernatural strength sweeping the planet. But how can anyone comprehend the devastation? The terror?

All these events immediately precede and accompany the return of Jesus Christ to save the city of Jerusalem and to fulfill His long-awaited promise to come again. I'm reminded of other passages in the Bible that make the same predictions.

Isaiah 29 paints a dramatic picture:

What sorrow awaits . . . the City of David. Year after year you celebrate your feasts. Yet I will bring disaster upon you, and there will be much weeping and sorrow. For Jerusalem will become what her name Ariel means—an altar covered with blood. . . . But suddenly, your ruthless enemies will be crushed like the finest of dust. Your many attackers will be driven away like chaff before the wind. Suddenly, in an instant, I, the LORD of Heaven's Armies, will act for you with thunder and earthquake and great noise, with whirlwind and storm and consuming fire. All the nations fighting against Jerusalem will vanish like a dream! Those who are attacking her walls will vanish like a vision in the night. (vv. 1–7 NLT)

This is precisely what Revelation predicts!
The prophet Ezekiel also foresaw these events, saying,

This is what will happen in that day: When Gog [the Antichrist] attacks the land of Israel, my hot anger will be aroused, declares the Sovereign LORD. In my zeal and fiery wrath I declare that at that time there shall be a great earthquake in the land of Israel. . . . The mountains will be overturned, the cliffs will crumble and every wall will fall to the ground. I will summon a sword against Gog on all my mountains, declares the Sovereign LORD. . . . I will pour down torrents of rain, hailstones and burning sulfur on him and on his troops and on the many nations with him. And so I will show my greatness and my holiness, and I will make myself known in the sight of many nations. (Ezekiel 38:18–23)

I'm amazed at the consistency of biblical prophecy. When we study the events of the last days, we can pull information from Isaiah, Daniel, Ezekiel, Zechariah, our Lord's sermon in Matthew 24–25, 1 and 2 Thessalonians and other writings of Paul, the last chapter of 2 Peter, and the book of Revelation. When we assemble the pieces, it all fits. Not everyone assembles the pieces exactly the same way, and different Bible teachers will differ on the details. But to me, the material is consistent, logical, and interlocking.

It all leads to this moment, the eve of our Lord's return, when the cities of the world collapse in heaps during the outpouring of the final bowl of wrath.

With the seventh bowl of wrath, the world's very underpinnings shudder and the foundations are removed. The great city of Babylon splits into three parts. Now, the lens of Revelation zooms in to have a closer look at the destruction of the city of Babylon and the system it represents. This is what occupies Revelation 17–18.

EVENT 41

# The Antichrist's Religiopolitical System Is Destroyed (17:1–18)

As I've said, Babylon is the code name for the global capital of the Antichrist. It may be a future city that is actually rebuilt on the site of the ruins of ancient Babylon. For a glimpse of how this might happen, look at the incredible new capital city of Naypyidaw, built almost secretly in Myanmar.[11] Though sparsely inhabited, it's six times the size of New York City and includes a vast system of highways, giant buildings, parks, and even a zoo. It sprang up in a remote region and the world hardly noticed.[12]

On the other hand, the future capital of the Antichrist may be an existing city such as the ones I previously mentioned. The title Babylon is biblical code for this city and its empire, which is opposed to God. From the book of Genesis onward, Babylon (Babel) has represented a system of human government in rebellion against the God of heaven. Babylon is mentioned about three hundred times in the Bible and is mentioned in Scripture more than any other city except Jerusalem.[13]

Babylon was founded by Nimrod in Genesis 10:8–10, and according to ancient lore,[14] Nimrod's wife established a false religion there. Elements of this false religion have entered into mythology and into many of the historic religions of this world.[15] The city of Babylon provides the backdrop for the events of the book of Daniel. It was the great city of Nebuchadnezzar and the home of the famous Hanging Gardens of Babylon.

In the 1980s, Saddam Hussein started rebuilding the city. He had his name inscribed on many of the bricks, envisioned the reconstruction of the city, built a fabulous modern palace there, and was ready to begin construction of cable cars over Babylon when war broke out.[16] Now Iraqi officials have reopened the site to tourists, and there is some talk that the United Nations has plans for restoring Babylon as an international site and cultural center.[17] But, of course, that may not currently be the safest place for a weekend junket.

Revelation 17 seems to describe the destruction of the political-religious system that emanates from Babylon. Chapter 18 describes the destruction of the actual city itself. These two aspects of Babylon are interrelated but somewhat different. Perhaps the best way to explain it is to ask what comes to our minds when we think about . . .

- Washington, DC? The government.
- Las Vegas? Gambling.
- Rome? The Vatican and Catholicism.
- Moscow? The Kremlin.
- Mecca? Islam.
- Bethlehem? The birth of Jesus.

There's much more to those cities, of course. But certain places become identified with the politics, culture, history, or socioeconomic systems based there. When it comes to Babylon, most commentators understand that Revelation 17 describes the collapse of the Antichrist's global systems (including his false religion) that are based in Babylon, and Revelation 18 describes the destruction of the actual city that serves as his global capital.

So let's begin with the strange description of the religious and economic conglomerate headquartered in Babylon. In Revelation 17:1, one of the angels said to John,

> *Come, I will show you the punishment of the great prostitute, who sits by many waters.*

The prostitute seems to represent the worldwide religiopolitical system centered in this city. The *many waters* represent a global dominion of this city, or globalism. We know this because verse 15 says,

> *The waters you saw, where the prostitute sits, are peoples, multitudes, nations and languages.*

The idea of prostitution often has a spiritual meaning in the Bible. We're to be committed to God like a godly person is committed to their spouse. We're to be exclusively His, with no other rivals in our hearts. We're to belong to God alone. Israel was the bride of Jehovah. The church is the bride of Christ.

Jeremiah said to the backslidden people of his day, "'But you have lived as a prostitute with many lovers—would you now return to me?' declares the LORD" (Jeremiah 3:1).

The apostle Paul told the Corinthians, "I am jealous for you with a godly jealousy. I promised you to one husband, to Christ, so that I might present you as a pure virgin to him" (2 Corinthians 11:2).

When something enters your life that you love more than your Lord, it's a form of unfaithfulness and spiritual harlotry. It is idolatry. The language here echoes a little-known passage from the Old Testament prophet Nahum, who said of the city of Nineveh, "Woe to the city of blood . . . ! Many casualties, piles of dead, bodies without number, people stumbling over corpses—all because of the wanton lust of a prostitute . . . who enslaved nations by her prostitution and peoples by her witchcraft" (Nahum 3:1–4).

It seems this prostitute is more than a city of bricks and steel. She represents the political and philosophical and religious system that is based in that city and which has deceived the world. Some scholars believe it represents a religion, such as radical Islam with its oil-rich territories. The Antichrist will use this prostitute but then discard her.

This keeps with the pattern of satanic activity in Revelation. Satan is trying to become like God by replicating God's plan, though all his efforts are twisted.

### Satan's Counterfeit Operation

- There is a false trinity.
  - There is a false father who possesses authority.
  - There is a false son who apparently dies and rises again.
  - There is a false spirit who seeks to glorify the false son.
- There is a false church or a false religion.
- There is a false city ("Babylon") to counter God's city of Jerusalem.

In simplest terms, we can say the prostitute woman in Revelation 17 represents the political-religious system centered in the capital city of Babylon. It is the Babel system. This is the ultimate anti-God empire, made up of evil human forces and evil supernatural principalities and powers. She is attached to the Antichrist (v. 3), very rich (v. 4), and a global source of abomination (v. 5). According to verse 6, she is *drunk with the blood of God's holy people, the blood of those who bore testimony to Jesus.*

In other words, she will be a huge part of the effort to track down, interrogate, torture, and slay those coming to Christ during the tribulation.

The loathsome woman (the false system of the Antichrist

centered in Babylon) is riding a scarlet beast covered with blasphemous names (the Antichrist). We're told this beast has seven heads and ten horns (v. 3). This was how the Antichrist was described when we met him in Revelation 13:1.

Now, in Revelation 17:10, we're told these seven heads represent seven kings:

> *Five have fallen, one is, and the other has not yet come; but when he does come, he must remain for only a little while.*

Commentators have different views about this, but many suggest this is referring to the seven great empires in biblical and world history as it relates to the ultimate plan of God. While many nations have risen and fallen during earth's convulsive history, the Bible focuses on a chain of empires that link the beginning of redemptive history with its end. The story of the exodus and the visions in Daniel 2 and 7 are foundational to what we read in Revelation and encompass the empires of:

1. Egypt, where Abraham's descendants sought refuge in famine and where they later became enslaved.
2. Assyria, one of Daniel's listed kingdoms, which destroyed the Northern Kingdom of Israel.
3. Babylon, the next in Daniel's list. Babylon destroyed the Southern Kingdom of Judah.
4. Medo-Persia, the next in Daniel's prophecies, which allowed a remnant of the Jewish people to return to their homeland and build the Second Temple.
5. Greece, which Daniel predicted and which flamed into history between the Old and New Testaments.
6. Rome, which Daniel also predicted in his prophecies and which destroyed the nation of Israel in AD 66–73.

7. The revival of the final world empire under the conqueror bent on conquest, revealed in the first seal in Revelation 6:2. This was also predicted by Daniel.

When the *conqueror bent on conquest* becomes infilled with Satan in the middle of the tribulation and suffers some kind of death and resurrection, he will become the Antichrist. In so doing, he will represent the eighth and final empire. Verse 11 says,

> *The beast who once was, and now is not, is an eighth king. He belongs to the seven and is going to his destruction.*

The beast not only had seven heads but ten horns, which are explained in Revelation 17:12–14:

> *The ten horns you saw are ten kings who have not yet received a kingdom, but who for one hour will receive authority as kings along with the beast. They have one purpose and will give their power and authority to the beast. They will wage war against the Lamb.*

These are the kings of the ten nations that compose the Antichrist's confederacy. They were predicted by Daniel in his image of the ten toes and ten horns (Daniel 2:41 and 7:7). This is the revived Roman Empire predicted in Daniel 2:42–45—the empire that has Babylon's hatred of God and Rome's lust for brutality.

In Revelation 17:16–18, the Antichrist and his ten-member confederation turn on the "prostitute" and destroy it. Verse 16 says,

> *The beast and the ten horns you saw will hate the prostitute. They will bring her to ruin and leave her naked; they will eat her flesh and burn her with fire.*

As his power is consolidated, the Antichrist will fling off the false religion that has helped finance his empire. Just to visualize this, suppose the Antichrist is a Russian despot who aligns himself with the Islamic oil-producing states, adopts Islam as his religion, and rakes in billions of dollars generated by oil. When he turns against Israel, he finds immediate support among radical Islamicists, but he doesn't want their interference anymore. He wants to be worshiped himself. He flings them off like an old jacket. He strips Islam of its wealth, then renounces and rejects it.

I'm not suggesting this is what will happen, so don't take my visualization as biblical truth. It's just a way of seeing the plausibility of this kind of scenario. One reason this story line interests me is because of the recent highly publicized predictions by certain Islamic agents who are expecting the arrival of the Mahdi, "the Rightly Guided One." According to Islamic belief, the apocalyptic messiah will appear at the end of world history, when the earth is engulfed in chaos, to establish a global Islamic kingdom and impose sharia law on the world.[18]

Let me, then, summarize this chapter. Leading up to and during the tribulation there will be a false religious-economic-sociopolitical system—maybe one of the world's great religions, maybe radical Islam, maybe apostate Catholicism or liberal Christianity, perhaps a new mythology, or perhaps a form of intolerant secularism, socialism, or atheism.

It will be based in the city code-named Babylon and will be of temporary use to the false trinity. But as the Antichrist consolidates his power, he will fling off this system so he can exercise unilateral power by himself.

Though Revelation 17 is rather difficult, I believe the main point is simple: as Jesus Christ prepares to return to earth, God will decimate the empire and the hideous operations of the Antichrist.

# The Antichrist's Capital City Implodes (18:1–24)

Chapter 18 is clearly devoted to the destruction of the capital city of Babylon itself and shows us in greater detail what will happen when the earthquake and global calamities strike her at the threshold of Christ's return.

Remember, God has His city, too—earthly Jerusalem. His ultimate capital is the heavenly Jerusalem, which we'll tour in the last two chapters of Revelation. But the Antichrist wants to exalt his city and his empire above those of the Lord—and that's his downfall.

How Satan wants to rival God! A false trinity. An Antichrist who dies and rises again. A false church. And a false capital city.

If chapter 17 has some difficult spots, chapter 18 is plain and simple—and catastrophic. It describes the destruction of the sprawling city of Babylon, capital of a global empire and the seat of power for the government of the Antichrist. This destruction occurs during the planetary earthquake described at the end of chapter 16, and here in chapter 18 the details are given, including the very words spoken by some who will witness the event.

In Revelation 18:1, John's angelic escort is arguably the most spectacular angel in the Bible. When he descends from heaven, the whole earth is illumined by his splendor. Remember that in some way the earth is in darkness, so the sight of this angel must be stunning, and a measure

*John's angelic escort is arguably the most spectacular angel in the Bible. When he descends from heaven, the whole earth is illumined by his splendor.*

of light returns to earth from his radiance. The angel is of very high rank and very powerful.

> *After this I saw another angel coming down from heaven. He had great authority, and the earth was illumined by his splendor. With a mighty voice he shouted.*

Imagine a shout heard around the world. The angel's message is a repetition of the pronouncement of Revelation 14:8:

> *Fallen! Fallen is Babylon the Great!*

Then he goes on to say,

> *She has become a dwelling for demons and a haunt for every impure spirit.* (v. 2)

During the tribulation, Babylon will become the center of activity for all the unseen dark forces, a city permeated with the principalities and powers of evil. These demonic forces will pervade the streets and alleys of Babylon and use it as a staging area for their global atrocities.

Babylon's affluence is mentioned in verse 3:

> *The merchants of the earth grew rich from her excessive luxuries.*

In verse 4, another angel shouts a warning to any underground believers, telling them to escape the city, as Lot escaped from Sodom. Apparently, some newly converted followers of the Lamb are hiding in the basements and alleys of Babylon, seeking to serve the Lord in the very center of global evil. Now they are told to flee.

*Then I heard another voice from heaven say: "'Come out of her, my people,' so that you will not share in her sins, so that you will not receive any of her plagues; for her sins are piled up to heaven, and God has remembered her crimes."*

The sentence of doom is then pronounced in verse 8:

*Therefore in one day her plagues will overtake her: death, mourning and famine. She will be consumed by fire, for mighty is the Lord God who judges her.*

As we watch the city begin to collapse, we notice three different groups of mourners watching it, all in a state of shock. First, the kings of the earth *will weep and mourn over her. Terrified at her torment, they will stand far off and cry: "'Woe! Woe to you, great city, you mighty city of Babylon! In one hour your doom has come!'"* (vv. 9–10).

I'm old enough to remember watching in disbelief as the Twin Towers of the World Trade Center collapsed. The world was glued to their television screens, and none of us could believe what we were seeing. Imagine that upheaval happening all over the world as the ground is shuddering, supervolcanoes are erupting, global cities are collapsing, and mammoth fires are raging.[19] It is the end of the world as we know it. The kings, generals, presidents, and premiers can only shake their heads and cry, "Woe."

Second, according to verses 11–16, the merchants of the earth will weep and mourn over Babylon because no one will ever buy their cargoes anymore—*cargoes of gold, silver, precious stones and pearls; fine linen, purple, silk and scarlet cloth; every sort of citron wood, and articles of every kind made of ivory, costly wood, bronze, iron and marble; cargoes of cinnamon and spice, of incense, myrrh and frankincense, of wine and olive oil, of fine flour and wheat; cattle and sheep; horses and carriages; and human beings sold as slaves* (vv. 12–13).

Notice the reality of slavery. That last item is as up-to-date as our headlines. This city had a lucrative trade in human trafficking with all its atrocious implications.

The third group of mourners are mariners and sea captains. Verses 17–18 say,

*Every sea captain, and all who travel by ship, the sailors, and all who earn their living from the sea, will stand far off. When they see the smoke of her burning, they will exclaim, "Was there ever a city like this great city?"*

All three groups of mourners—political leaders, business leaders, and seafaring traders—are astounded that a vast city like Babylon can be reduced to rubble in just one single hour.

But while the leaders of the world are crying "Woe," another group is shouting, "Rejoice!"

Verse 20 says,

*Rejoice over her, you heavens! Rejoice, you people of God! Rejoice, apostles and prophets! For God has judged her with the judgment she imposed on you.*

Then in verse 21 as an act of finality, a mighty angel picks up a millstone and hurls it into the sea, symbolically affirming the total destruction of the city. The angel speaks this poignant epithet over the smoldering ruins of the world's greatest metropolis:

*With such violence the great city of Babylon will be thrown down, never to be found again. The music of harpists and musicians, pipers and trumpeters, will never be heard in you again. No worker of any trade will ever be found in you again. The sound of a millstone will never be heard in you again. The light of a lamp will never shine in you again. The voice of bridegroom and bride will never be heard in you again. Your merchants were the world's important people. By your magic spell all the nations were led astray. In her was found the blood of prophets and of God's holy people, of all who have been slaughtered on the earth.* (18:21–24)

Now at last, it is time for the Lord Jesus Christ—who is King of kings and Lord of lords, who is the Lion and the Lamb, who once came to earth as a baby in a manger—to return as a mighty Warrior to save His people and bring the drama of the ages to its fitting, God-decreed consummation.

# The Return of Christ
## Revelation 19–22

I hope you're grasping my idea that the book of Revelation is understandable to any follower of Christ who simply takes the events as they come. We can always go back and study the details, compare John's writings with critical Old Testament passages, glance at commentaries on Revelation, and grow in our grasp of its meaning. But grasping its simplicity gives us a starting point for digging deeper.

The apostle John was exiled to the island of Patmos, where he was allowed to see a vision of the glorified Christ (Revelation 1). The Lord Jesus gave him a personal word for seven specific churches to whom John ministered (Revelation 2–3). Then John was transported to the great throne room of God where, in a great worship environment, Jesus Christ was appointed to begin the process of drawing the history of the world toward a conclusion (Revelation 4–5). For seven years, the world writhed in its death pains (Revelation 6–18), with the devil and his host turning their full fury on Israel, perhaps in an attempt to thwart the return of Christ.

The first half of this period is described in chapters 6–11. The dramatic midpoint is found in chapters 12–13. The violent last half of the tribulation runs from Revelation 14 to 18. The armies of the world surrounded Jerusalem, and the city was besieged.

Just as the Holy City teeters on the brink of total military collapse, at that exact moment Jesus Christ will return as He promised, in the clouds of glory, in splendor, in power, to claim the victory. Revelation 19 describes the return of Christ. Chapter 20 describes His earthly reign of one thousand years, followed by the great white throne judgment. The final two chapters of the Bible—Revelation 21–22—are our priceless travel guide to our eternal home.

## The Tribulation

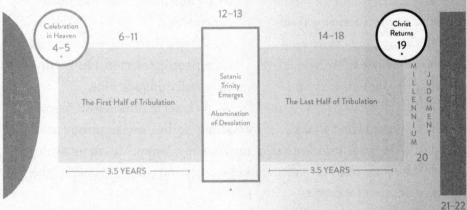

# Hallelujahs Ring Out
# in Heaven (19:1–10)

In contrast to earth's dying groans and wails, God's heaven of heavens suddenly breaks into hallelujahs of praise never before heard in history—the true "Hallelujah Chorus." Think of the most intense and pulsating music you've ever heard, then multiply that by a billion.

The word *hallelujah* is found sparingly in the Bible. It's reserved for only the most sacred occasions. It occurs a few times in the Psalms and four times in the New Testament—all four times in this chapter. Each hallelujah represents a new burst or anthem of heavenly praise.

At this moment in the unfolding events of Revelation, Jesus Christ is stepping from His throne, ready to descend from the vault of the heavens and from the unseen realms. The hour has come for Him to enter the smoldering globe and rescue His people—Israel and any surviving Christ-followers—and to bring the battle of Armageddon to a sudden halt and a victorious conclusion.

*Jesus Christ is stepping from His throne, ready to descend from the vault of the heavens and from the unseen realms.*

The first time He came, His own people rejected Him. Now they will embrace Him.

When He came the first time, He came as a babe wrapped in swaddling clothes, and near the end of His life He rode into Jerusalem on a donkey. When He comes again, He'll be dressed in the vestments of victory and riding, as it were, the white horse of victory.

When He came the first time, there was no room in the inn. When He comes again, the whole world will be His domain.

He came the first time to be crucified. He will come again to be glorified.

He came the first time as the Author of our salvation. He will come again as the Finisher of our faith.

His first coming was known only to a few shepherds, a handful of wise men, and a few residents of Bethlehem. When He comes again, it will be as lightning flashing from the east to the west; He will come in the clouds of glory, and all the universe will hear the news.

When He came at Bethlehem, the angels sang, "Glory to God in the highest" (Luke 2:14). When He comes again, they will sing, "Hallelujah! For our Lord God Almighty reigns" (Revelation 19:6).

Try to imagine the scene. As the capital city of Babylon burns in its ashes and the great cities of the world implode in clouds of dust and disaster, the Antichrist and the armies of the earth will be on the verge of total victory over Israel and its ancient capital of Jerusalem.

From their staging area north of Israel in the Armageddon plains, the massed armies are moments away from total control, perhaps scaling the ancient limestone blocks of the temple complex. Jerusalem has been ravaged but has not yet fallen. God has caused global plagues and a worldwide series of unimaginable cataclysms and earthquakes to disrupt all Satan is trying to do. While a segment of the population is hiding in a secret location, their friends and loved ones are facing unimaginable terror and Jerusalem is on the verge of total military defeat.

The moment is now at hand toward which all history has been lunging from the days of Adam, Abraham, and the patriarchs, from the days of Moses and the exodus, from the days of Israel and the prophets, from the days of the Gospels and of the church and its global mission.

As Jesus stands in His real, resurrected, and glorified body and prepares to descend to earth, all heaven bursts into praise so intense and so sustained that the entire universe reverberates.

Revelation 19:1–7 says,

*"Hallelujah! Salvation and glory and power belong to our God, for true and just are his judgments. He has condemned the great prostitute who corrupted the earth by her adulteries. He has avenged on her the blood of his servants." . . .*

*The twenty-four elders and the four living creatures fell down and worshiped God, who was seated on the throne. And they cried:*

*"Amen, Hallelujah!"*

*Then a voice came from the throne, saying,*

*"Praise our God, all you his servants, you who fear him, both great and small!"*

*Then I heard what sounded like a great multitude, like the roar of rushing waters and like loud peals of thunder, shouting:*

*"Hallelujah! For our Lord God Almighty reigns. Let us rejoice and be glad and give him glory! For the wedding of the Lamb has come, and his bride has made herself ready."*

Jesus is about to be united with His redeemed people of all the ages—including His own people, Israel, who are about to turn to Him en masse.

This will be the Wedding Supper of the Lamb.

In the Bible, sharing a meal with God is a big deal. In Genesis 18, Abraham shared a meal with God. In Exodus 24, Moses and the leaders of Israel ascended Mount Sinai and "they saw God, and they ate and drank" (v. 11). This was a covenant meal, part of the celebration of the giving of the law. In the Gospels, Jesus shared the Last Supper with His disciples and established the Lord's Supper with them. After the resurrection, He sat down at the supper table with two disciples on the road to Emmaus (Luke 24:30). Suppers were celebratory moments of significance and fellowship.

Jesus is returning to celebrate with His people forever. The Wedding Supper of the Lamb is a synonym and symbol of the return of Christ, when He will be with His people and eat and drink with them forever.

Later in the chapter, we'll read about another feast, as the animals and birds of prey feed on the dead bodies of the fallen enemies. But the song of the angels is announcing the Wedding Supper of the Lamb, the greatest moment in human history for those who know Christ. It was previewed by Isaiah like this:

> On this mountain the LORD Almighty will prepare a feast of rich food for all peoples, a banquet of aged wine. . . . On this mountain he will destroy the shroud that enfolds all peoples, the sheet that covers all nations; he will swallow up death forever. The Sovereign LORD will wipe away the tears from all faces; he will remove his people's disgrace from all the earth. The LORD has spoken. In that day they will say, "Surely this is . . . the LORD, we trusted in him; let us rejoice and be glad in his salvation." (Isaiah 25:6–9)

EVENT 44

# The Lord Jesus Christ Returns! (19:11–16)

Now we're here! An enormous flash of lightning tears through the sky from east to west, ripping the heavens apart (Matthew 24:27), and John said,

> *I saw heaven standing open and there before me was a white horse, whose rider is called Faithful and True. With justice he judges and wages war. His eyes are like blazing fire, and on his head are many crowns. He has a name written on him that no one knows but he himself. He is dressed in a robe dipped in blood, and his name is the Word of God. The armies of heaven were following him, riding on white horses and dressed in fine linen, white and clean. Coming out*

*of his mouth is a sharp sword with which to strike down the nations.
"He will rule them with an iron scepter." He treads the winepress of
the fury of the wrath of God Almighty. On his robe and on his thigh
he has this name written: king of kings and lord of lords. (19:11–18)*

From heaven, John saw the Lamb of God, pictured symbolically
as a rider on a white horse. His names are listed: Faithful and True,
the Word of God, King of kings and Lord of lords. The angelic
armies are following Him, and He descends to the earth with a
sharp sword coming out of His mouth.

This isn't a literal sword. It's symbolic of the power of the words
of Jesus. Our Lord will win the battle of Armageddon with nothing
more than the words of His mouth. The one who said, "Let there be
light," and "Blessed are the poor," and "What is impossible with man
is possible with God" will channel His omnipotent power through
the tone of His voice and the sound of His syllables (Genesis 1:3;
Matthew 5:3; Luke 18:27).

Our Lord's power is often conveyed by His thoughts and voice.
He spoke and Lazarus came forth. He spoke and the storm was
stilled. The man in the New Testament who said, "Lord, just say
the word, and my servant will be healed" understood the power of
Jesus' voice and was commended for his faith (Matthew 8:8). The
soul is saved and our lives are transformed by listening to His Word.

Jesus' great weapon at the battle of Armageddon is simply His voice.
Out of His mouth comes a sharp sword with which to strike the
nations. The power of His voice will repel and vaporize His foes.

Remember what Martin Luther said about the devil?

"One little word shall fell him."[1]

This is also taught in 2 Thessalonians 2:8: "And then the lawless one [the Antichrist] will be revealed, whom the Lord Jesus will overthrow with the breath of his mouth and destroy by the splendor of his coming."

I believe this is also the moment of Israel's national conversion to Christ. Let me take you back to Zechariah 12:9–10 and 13:1.

On that day I will set out to destroy all the nations that attack Jerusalem. And I will pour out on the house of David and the inhabitants of Jerusalem a spirit of grace and supplication. They will look on me, the one they have pierced, and they will mourn for him as one mourns for an only child, and grieve bitterly for him as one grieves for a firstborn son. . . . On that day a fountain will be opened to the house of David and the inhabitants of Jerusalem, to cleanse them from sin and impurity.

The prophet Ezekiel spoke richly about this. In his vision of the valley of dry bones, he described the political reestablishing of the nation of Israel (which we saw in 1948), picturing it as dry bones coming together and being covered with flesh. But later, he said, the reviving breath of God will enter into them and they will come to life and stand as a vast army, spiritually brought to life. "I will put my Spirit in you and you will live . . ." (Ezekiel 37:14).

". . . and in this way all Israel will be saved" (Romans 11:26).

Just before His death, Jesus looked out over the city He loved—Jerusalem—and said, "For I tell you, you will not see me again until you say, 'Blessed is he who comes in the name of the Lord'" (Matthew 23:39).

Jewish soldiers facing massacre will look heavenward, see Him, and cry, "Blessed is He who comes in the name of the Lord!" Nursing mothers and children trapped in the horrors of urban warfare will see the flash of His coming and shout, "Blessed is He who comes in the name of the Lord! Hosanna in the highest!"

Oh, what a day! The national conversion of the sons and

daughters of Abraham, the descendants of David, the tribes of Israel, the redeemed nation of Israel!

The prophet Zechariah told us how the return of Jesus will look from ground level. Let's look at Zechariah 14:3–5, which fills out the picture of Revelation 19. As you read, remember that in Acts 1, Jesus ascended into heaven from the Mount of Olives, and two nearby angels told the disciples He would return in the same way.

Every time I visit Israel, I spend time wandering around the Mount of Olives, the mountain ridge to the east of the Old City of Jerusalem and separated from it by the fabled Kidron Valley. Today a large cemetery and many different houses, hotels, shops, and religious sites cover the Mount of Olives, along with a few patches of old olive trees. But somewhere in that area is the very spot from which Jesus ascended to heaven, and this will be the place where His feet touch down. When He lands He will do so with the force of an earthquake.

Here is the aforementioned Zechariah 14:3–5:

> Then the LORD will go out and fight against those nations, as he fights on a day of battle. On that day his feet will stand on the Mount of Olives, east of Jerusalem, and the Mount of Olives will be split in two from east to west, forming a great valley, with half of the mountain moving north and half moving south. You will flee by my mountain valley, for it will extend to Azel.

As the forces of the Antichrist bulldoze their way west to east toward the Temple Mount with more forces pouring in from the north and south and east, the Jewish people will be trapped around the temple. Jerusalem will be trampled underfoot by the armies of the Gentiles.

At that moment, Jesus will appear in the sky. Matthew 24:30 says, "Then will appear the sign of the Son of Man in heaven. And then all the peoples of the earth will mourn when they see the Son of Man coming on the clouds of heaven, with power and great glory."

He will descend to the Mount of Olives and the earth will crack beneath Him, forming a valley through the Olivet Ridge and providing escape to the trapped Jewish people as Jesus enters the Eastern Gate and turns His attention to the invading hordes.

Those who believe the rapture and resurrection of the church will occur at the moment of Jesus' return view this as the moment when the graves give up their dead. If this is the moment Paul referred to in 1 Thessalonians 4 and 1 Corinthians 15, at this very moment billions of bodies will fly like skyrockets into the air, suddenly glorified, and will join Jesus as He descends. The living followers of Christ will be caught up and transformed in the flash of an eye to become part of the heavenly invasion to liberate a satanically held world.

Notice how these events in Revelation 17–19 perfectly fulfill Jesus' predictions in Luke 21:20–28:

> When you see Jerusalem being surrounded by armies, you will know that its desolation is near. Then let those who are in Judea flee to the mountains, let those in the city get out, and let those in the country not enter the city. For this is the time of punishment in fulfillment of all that has been written. How dreadful it will be in those days for pregnant women and nursing mothers! There will be great distress in the land and wrath against this people. They will fall by the sword and will be taken as prisoners to all the nations. Jerusalem will be trampled on by the Gentiles until the times of the Gentiles are fulfilled.
>
> There will be signs in the sun, moon and stars. On the earth, nations will be in anguish and perplexity at the roaring and tossing of the sea. People will faint from terror, apprehensive of what is coming on the world, for the heavenly bodies will be shaken. At that time they will see the Son of Man coming in a cloud with power and great glory. When these things begin to take place, stand up and lift up your heads, because your redemption is drawing near.

# The Rebels Are
# Defeated (19:17–21)

The last paragraphs of Revelation 19 describe the incredible victory gained by Jesus and the armies of heaven. As Jesus descends, the Antichrist and all his armies suddenly turn their fire on Him, to no avail.

*And I saw an angel standing in the sun, who cried in a loud voice to all the birds flying in midair, "Come, gather together for the great supper of God, so that you may eat the flesh of kings, generals, and the mighty, of horses and their riders, and the flesh of all people, free and slave, great and small."*

*Then I saw the beast and the kings of the earth and their armies gathered together to wage war against the rider on the horse and his army. But the beast was captured, and with it the false prophet who had performed the signs on its behalf. With these signs he had deluded those who had received the mark of the beast and worshiped its image. The two of them were thrown alive into the fiery lake of burning sulfur. The rest were killed with the sword coming out of the mouth of the rider on the horse, and all the birds gorged themselves on their flesh.* (vv. 17–21)

On the night before Christ's crucifixion, a contingent of Roman soldiers came to arrest Him. Jesus saw the troops with their torches and drawn swords, and He said, "Who is it you want?" They told Him they were looking for Jesus of Nazareth, to which Jesus said, "I am He." At that moment, the soldiers were struck with an invisible blast radiating from His words that propelled them backward, knocking them to the ground (John 18:4–6). On that occasion,

Jesus withdrew His power and allowed Himself to be arrested. But when He comes again, the force of His words will send His enemies reeling backward like twigs in a tornado. Daniel 2:35 says they will be "like chaff on a threshing floor in the summer. The wind swept them away." The shock waves from His very presence will repel the rebels and instantly secure an unconditional victory.

In Daniel 8:23–25, the end of the lawless one is pictured like this:

> *When Jesus comes again, the force of His words will send His enemies reeling backward like twigs in a tornado.*

> [A] fierce-looking king, a master of intrigue, will arise. He will become very strong, but not by his own power. He will cause astounding devastation and will succeed in whatever he does. He will destroy those who are mighty, the holy people. He will cause deceit to prosper, and he will consider himself superior. When they feel secure, he will destroy many and take his stand against the Prince of princes. Yet he will be destroyed, but not by human power.

This is also in keeping with the prophecy of Ezekiel, who said about the Antichrist, "Then I will strike your bow from your left hand and make your arrows drop from your right hand. On the mountains of Israel you will fall, you and all your troops and the nations with you. I will give you as food to all kinds of carrion birds and to the wild animals" (Ezekiel 39:3–4).

Daniel said, "In the time of those kings [the coalition of forces under the Antichrist], the God of heaven will set up a kingdom that will never be destroyed. . . . It will crush all those kingdoms and bring them to an end, but it will itself endure forever" (Daniel 2:44).

Isaiah described this moment like this: "For he will come like a pent-up flood that the breath of the LORD drives along. 'The Redeemer will come to Zion, to those in Jacob who repent of their sins'" (Isaiah 59:19–20).

We're told it will take seven months to bury all the bodies and cleanse the land. Huge mass graves will fill the Valley of Hamon Gog, and the survivors of Israel will use the discarded weapons for firewood and fuel for the next seven years (Ezekiel 39:9–12).

EVENT 46

# The Millennium Breaks Forth (20:1–3)

What will happen next? That brings us to event 46—the millennium, or the thousand-year reign of Christ. In the unfolding sequence of events in Revelation, this follows in logical order:

> *And I saw an angel coming down out of heaven, having the key to the Abyss and holding in his hand a great chain. He seized the dragon, that ancient serpent, who is the devil, or Satan, and bound him for a thousand years. He threw him into the Abyss, and locked and sealed it over him, to keep him from deceiving the nations anymore.* (20:1–3)

The Abyss, remember, is the God-built supermax prison. Here Satan will reside for a thousand years. Interestingly, the Antichrist and the False Prophet are already in another place, known as *the fiery lake of burning sulfur*, which we commonly call "hell" (Revelation 19:20). Satan will eventually end up there too.

For now, he is captured, separated from his two accomplices, and imprisoned in the dreaded Abyss.

The phrase *thousand years* occurs six times in this passage, which is why we call this period the millennium, a Latin term referring to a thousand years (*mille + annum*). I don't know of any good way to interpret this except literally. Other time designations in Revelation (42 months, 3.5 years, 1,260 days) seem to be literal.

I believe this millennium is a thousand-year earthly reign of Jesus Christ on this planet following His return. During this time, earth will not be perfect or sinless. This isn't the new heaven and the new earth. It's not our heavenly home. It's not the eternal state, but it's a preview of the eternal state.

During this time Satan will be bound, and Jesus will literally be reigning and ruling. It will be a theocratic kingdom. The Jewish people will grow and flourish. The survivors of the tribulation will replenish the earth, and during this time God will fulfill all His Old Testament promises to the nation of Israel.

The prophet Isaiah said, "I will send some of those who survive to the nations—to Tarshish, to the Libyans and Lydians (famous as archers), to Tubal and Greece, and to the distant islands that have not heard of my fame or seen my glory. They will proclaim my glory among the nations" (Isaiah 66:19).

This is a major theme of Scripture. Dr. J. Dwight Pentecost wrote, "A larger body of prophetic Scripture is devoted to the subject of the millennium, developing its character and conditions, than any other subject."[2]

Habakkuk spoke of this period of history when he wrote, "For the earth will be filled with the knowledge of the glory of the Lord as the waters cover the sea" (Habakkuk 2:14).

The final chapter of Zechariah tells us that when Jesus returns to the Mount of Olives, the earth beneath Him will crack open, unleashing underground springs that will flow like rivers into the Dead Sea and into the Mediterranean Sea, turning Israel into a land like the garden of Eden (Zechariah 14:8).

"The Lord will be king over the whole earth. On that day there will be one Lord, and his name the only name" (v. 9).

The last chapters of Ezekiel also describe the altered geography of

> *When Jesus returns to the Mount of Olives, the earth beneath Him will crack open, unleashing underground springs that will flow like rivers.*

Jerusalem and the wonderful Millennial Temple, to which the glory of the Lord returns as in Old Testament days. From beneath the temple, a river flows down to the Dead Sea, turning it into a paradise: "The salty water there becomes fresh. . . . There will be large numbers of fish, because this water flows there and makes the salt water fresh. . . . Fishermen will stand along the shore. . . . Fruit trees of all kinds will grow on both banks of the river" (47:8–12).

This is what Isaiah, son of Amoz, saw concerning Judah and Jerusalem:

> In the last days the mountain of the LORD's temple will be established as the highest of the mountains; it will be exalted above the hills, and all nations will stream to it. Many peoples will come and say, "Come, let us go up to the mountain of the LORD, to the temple of the God of Jacob. He will teach us his ways, so that we may walk in his paths." The law will go out from Zion, the word of the LORD from Jerusalem. He will judge between the nations and will settle disputes for many peoples. They will beat their swords into plowshares and their spears into pruning hooks. Nation will not take up sword against nation, nor will they train for war anymore. (Isaiah 2:1–4)

EVENT 47

# The Tribulation Saints Are Resurrected to Reign with Christ (20:4–6)

Who will help Jesus rule the earth? All those who had been martyred during the seven years of tribulation. They are resurrected to serve as kings, presidents, governors, mayors, and leaders on the new earth.

*I saw thrones on which were seated those who had been given authority to judge. And I saw the souls of those who had been beheaded because of their testimony about Jesus and because of the word of God. They had not worshiped the beast or its image and had not received its mark on their foreheads or their hands. They came to life and reigned with Christ a thousand years.* (20:4)

This is fascinating. Who will populate the earth during the millennium? Two groups: (1) the surviving newly converted Jewish people who will live in Israel and grow in numbers and (2) those who survive the tribulation. Zechariah 14:16–18 says,

Then the survivors from all the nations that have attacked Jerusalem will go up year after year to worship the King, the LORD Almighty, and to celebrate the Festival of Tabernacles. If any of the peoples of the earth do not go up to Jerusalem to worship the King, the LORD Almighty, they will have no rain. If the Egyptian people do not go up and take part, they will have no rain. The LORD will bring on them the plague he inflicts on the nations that do not go up to celebrate the Festival of Tabernacles.

There could be thousands upon thousands of people who come to Christ during the seven years of distress and manage to survive the dragnets of the Antichrist. In 1 Kings 19, Elijah thought he was the only believer still alive in Israel as he himself was being hunted down for slaughter. But the Lord told him, "Yet I reserve seven thousand in Israel—all whose knees have not bowed down to Baal and whose mouths have not kissed him" (v. 18).

In the same way, perhaps God will preserve thousands of people who come to Christ during the tribulation and whose lives will be providentially hidden, as it were, from the Antichrist's agents. These survivors will repopulate the earth, with so many babies born that a population explosion will occur. Zechariah 8:4–5 says of this period, "Once again men and women of ripe old age will sit in the streets of Jerusalem, each of them with cane in hand because of their age. The city streets will be filled with boys and girls playing there."

Isaiah described the millennium like this:

I will create Jerusalem to be a delight and its people a joy. . . . Never again will there be in it an infant who lives but a few days, or an old man who does not live out his years; the one who dies at a hundred will be thought a mere child. . . . They will build houses and dwell in them; they will plant vineyards and eat their fruit. . . . They will not labor in vain, nor will they bear children doomed to misfortune; for they will be a people blessed by the Lord, they and their descendants with them. . . . The wolf and the lamb will feed together, and the lion eat straw like the ox. . . . They will neither harm nor destroy on all my holy mountain. (Isaiah 65:18–25)

Many of my friends believe we'll be on earth with Christ during the millennium, and they may be right. I tend to believe we'll be enjoying the great city of New Jerusalem in our resurrected and glorified bodies. In other words, I expect to be in heaven during the earthly reign of Christ, not on this planet.

The population of the millennium will be made up of believing survivors of the tribulation who will marry, procreate, and replenish the earth. They will grow old and some will die, though the lifespans will be similar to those described at the beginning of Genesis—perhaps hundreds of years. Satan will be bound during this period, but humans will still have the stain of sin within them. And within a thousand years, the world will again be ready to rebel against the Lord Jesus.

That doesn't sound like a place for glorified saints.

But if we're in heaven while Christ is on earth, won't we be separated from Him?

First, there's nothing to prevent Christ from traveling instantly from His heavenly throne to His earthly throne. We would expect Him to do so. I don't believe He will vacate His heavenly throne the same as He did during His first coming. He will be ruling and reigning in both heaven and earth.

Second, as we've discussed before, a thousand years in God's sight is like a day (2 Peter 3:8), so our separation from Him would be fleeting at most.

Third, His presence will fill heaven and earth, and this is a mystery I can't fully explain, which is a good thing. As I've often read and said, a Savior small enough to understand isn't big enough to be worshiped.

Fourth, when Revelation 20:4 says, *They came to life and reigned with Christ a thousand years*, it isn't referring to all believers in history but to the martyrs of the tribulation. And finally, who can limit what the Lord wants to do? I cannot answer every question. The Lord gives us some rich information about these times but not total knowledge. Even with all the prophecies God has given us, there is much that is veiled in glorious mystery. Christ still has wonderful surprises ahead for us! I simply want to be wherever He desires.

EVENT 48

# The Final Battle (20:7–10)

Even with Satan bound, the sinful nature of humanity will break through by the end of the thousand years. The population of earth will be teeming once again, and Satan will be released. There will be some sort of recurrence of the battle of Armageddon—of Gog and Magog, as we saw in Revelation 16.

*When the thousand years are over, Satan will be released from his prison and will go out to deceive the nations in the four corners of the earth—Gog and Magog—and to gather them for battle. In number they are like the sand on the seashore. They marched across the breadth of the earth and surrounded the camp of God's people, the city he loves. But fire came down from heaven and devoured them. And the devil, who deceived them, was thrown into the lake of burning sulfur, where the beast and the false prophet had been thrown. They will be tormented day and night for ever and ever. (20:7–10)*

Why is Satan released at all? Dr. W. A. Criswell in his commentary of Revelation answers the only way possible. He wrote, "We now come to a revelation in the Word of God that I cannot understand. I do not think any man can understand it. There is something here that lies beyond human comprehension. . . . We cannot fathom it. It belongs to the secret counsels of Heaven."[3]

EVENT 49

# The Wicked Are Judged at the Great White Throne (20:11–15)

The last half of Revelation 20 contains the single most frightening passage of the entire Bible. At the end of the millennium and after the final battle, our eyes fall across the words of Revelation 20:11:

*Then I saw a great white throne and him who was seated on it. The earth and the heavens fled from his presence.*

This may be the point where the present heavens and earth are dissolved in fire, as Peter predicted when he said,

The present heavens and earth are reserved for fire, being kept for the day of judgment and destruction of the ungodly. . . . The heavens will disappear with a roar; the elements will be destroyed by fire, and the earth and everything done in it will be laid bare. . . . That day will bring about the destruction of the heavens by fire, and the elements will melt in the heat. But in keeping with his promise we are looking forward to a new heaven and a new earth, where righteousness dwells. (2 Peter 3:7, 10, 12–13)

The last thing that will happen before the universe blazes and melts into nonexistence is the resurrection of all the unbelieving dead of all the ages—all who rejected God's plan of redemption by grace. Up to this point they have moldered in their graves.

The Bible presents the process of resurrection as occurring in stages. First came the resurrection of Christ on Easter Sunday; then of the saints of all the ages at the rapture, whenever that occurs; then the tribulation saints who are destined to reign with Christ during the millennium. All these are said to be part of a *first resurrection*—the resurrection to life (Revelation 20:5).

God, in His mercy, spares the wicked dead until the very end. Now they are resurrected and suspended before a holy Judge as the entire cosmos recedes into nothingness. This throne is not the throne of grace. There is no diamond beauty, no rainbow of mercy. It is a blinding throne of burning white. It is *great* for it represents unrivaled authority; and it is *white*, which symbolizes unflinching purity.

Revelation 20:12 says,

*And I saw the dead, great and small, standing before the throne, and books were opened.*

Evidently these books contain the life histories of all those who have ever lived.

Verse 12 continues:

*Another book was opened, which is the book of life.*

The Book of Life, or the Lamb's Book of Life, seems to be a record of every person who Christ has ever redeemed. Revelation 21:27 says of heaven,

*But nothing unclean will ever enter it, nor anyone who does what is detestable or false, but only those who are written in the Lamb's book of life.* (ESV)

According to Revelation 17:8, this book has existed *from the creation of the world.*

The apostle Paul referred to this book in Philippians 4:3, saying, "Help these women since they have contended at my side in the cause of the gospel, along with Clement and the rest of my co-workers, whose names are in the book of life."

Jesus told His disciples, "However, do not rejoice that the spirits submit to you, but rejoice that your names are written in heaven" (Luke 10:20).

The moment a person receives Jesus Christ as Savior, their name is recorded in the Lamb's book; or, perhaps the names in this book are foreknown to God and recorded before the foundation of the world (Revelation 13:8 ESV). How terrible to stand before the blazing glory of God while angels search the records for your name, to no avail! The terror of this scene defies imagination.

Verses 12–15 continue:

*The dead were judged according to what they had done as recorded in the books. The sea gave up the dead that were in it, and death and Hades gave up the dead that were in them, and each person was*

*judged according to what they had done. Then death and Hades were thrown into the lake of fire. The lake of fire is the second death. Anyone whose name was not found written in the book of life was thrown into the lake of fire.*

As the last person descends into judgment, the history of planet earth is closed and concluded forever. The last moment has come.

The book of Revelation is filled with apocalyptic events, but this is the most somber, most unnerving scene. If you're reading this with an uncertain heart about your relationship with the Savior who died to save you from this moment, I urge you to put this book down at once, fall to your knees, and sincerely pray for Jesus Christ to enter your life with His life-changing forgiveness, grace, and abundance. At the back of this book, I've put a guide to the gospel message and a simple prayer you can pray in response to it.

This passage always leaves a deep and heavy burden on my heart for those who aren't serious about following Jesus Christ, and it motivates me to share the gospel whenever and however I can.

## The Tribulation

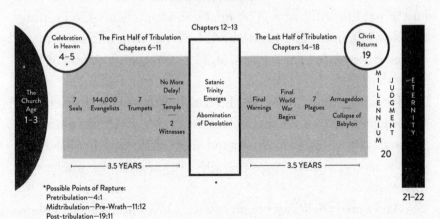

# The New Heaven, the New Earth, the New Jerusalem— and Eternity! (21:1–22:21)

The great white throne judgment is the final event in God's calendar of the end times of the old earth. Now we turn the page, come to chapters 21–22, and find that we're in the land of eternity, the everlasting Eden—paradise!

Revelation 21 opens with the creation of a glorious new universe and an imperishable world for the redeemed of all the ages. I enjoy letting the scenes from these two chapters fill my mind, and I often ponder them when I'm falling asleep at night. Whenever I think of my dear wife, Katrina, who now resides in this city, I'm filled with joy. How wonderful of God to close His Book to us with these incredible forty-eight verses!

The spiritual and physical realms will merge, and our enjoyment of eternal life will begin. The final two chapters are God's *Travel Guide to Eternity*. The Lord ends His Bible with a description of the new heaven, the new earth, and His everlasting capital of New Jerusalem.

I've long wanted to write a book about these two chapters, but other people have done that better than I can. So let me guide you through the verses as I understand them, following my basic rule that whatever makes sense literally can plausibly be interpreted that way.

And I take these two chapters with a lot of literalness! I believe God gave these descriptions to us so we can visualize the scenes and anticipate our inheritance.

Revelation 21:1 says,

*Then I saw "a new heaven and a new earth," for the first heaven and the first earth had passed away, and there was no longer any sea.*

Some scholars believe the old heavens and earth will be melted down and recast, similar to the way our old bodies will decay then be resurrected and glorified, imperishable, and equipped for eternity. Others believe this is a totally new universe made from scratch at the spoken command from God (ex nihilo)—a new creation, and, of course, glorified, imperishable, and equipped for eternity.

In either case, the new heaven refers to a new universe, a new cosmos, to intergalactic space. If our current galaxies are mind-boggling, think of the eternal galaxies that will make up the new heaven.

*If our current galaxies are mind-boggling, think of the eternal galaxies that will make up the new heaven.*

Suspended somewhere in God's new, big, and beautiful universe will be a brand-new planet earth. Yes, God is going to create a new earth as our eternal home.

The new earth will be much larger, in my opinion, than the current earth. I have several reasons for believing that. First, we know God can create enormous planets. In our present solar system, Jupiter is more than ten times the size of earth. Second, you would expect our eternal home to be enormous. It will be the home for billions and billions of people, plus all the angels. And third, the city of New Jerusalem is said to be 1,400 miles high.[4] To put that in perspective, the space station orbits about 248 miles above the earth.[5] Imagine a city with its highest spires over a thousand miles beyond the space station! The size of planet earth will need to be proportional to the size of its capital city, which is enormous.

Perhaps you're disappointed there will be no more sea, but I'm certain there will be enormous and beautiful bodies of water. From the current earth, we can learn that God loves all kinds of water features in His creative planning. But today about 70 percent of the planet is covered with salty water—a vast wasteland in regard to normal human habitation. For John, the Aegean Sea isolated him from those he loved the most. While there will surely be beautiful bodies of water, I expect much more of the new earth will be inhabitable.[6]

In 2 Corinthians 12, the apostle Paul spoke of a time when he had been "caught up to the third heaven, . . . to paradise." He "heard inexpressible things, things that no one is permitted to tell" (vv. 2–4). The first heaven is the blue sky above our heads, the second is the universe beyond, and the third is the heaven of heavens where God dwells. The word *paradise* is an old Persian word that conveys the idea of royal gardens.[7] Paul received a glimpse of what John saw in Revelation. Paul wasn't allowed to describe what he saw, for God had another message for him to give—the gospel. But now John was allowed, even commanded, to describe for us the wonderful sights and sounds. Having seen the new universe and the new earth, his attention was drawn to something high above him, descending through the stars and through the skies like a gigantic and glorious gemstone.

Revelation 21:2 says,

*I saw the Holy City, the new Jerusalem, coming down out of heaven from God, prepared as a bride beautifully dressed for her husband.*

The Holy City exists now. It's somewhere above our heads in an unseen realm. I believe it currently serves as God's capital city, the home of His throne, of His angelic hosts, and of all those who have died in Jesus. When my wife passed away, I believe she was transported to this great city, where she probably received a temporary body (or an image of one) until her resurrected body will catch up to her.

This city has been on the minds of God's people from the very beginning. The Bible says Abraham "was looking forward to the city with foundations, whose architect and builder is God" (Hebrews 11:10). The Old Testament heroes and prophets "were longing for a better country—a heavenly one. Therefore God is not ashamed to be called their God, for he has prepared a city for them" (Hebrews 11:16).

Hebrews 13:14 says, "For here we do not have an enduring city, but we are looking for the city that is to come."

Think of it! There is an eternal city with foundations (we'll see those in the next few verses) and Almighty God is the architect and builder. He has prepared this city for His people, and we should long for it. On the last night of His natural earthly life, Jesus said, "I am going there to prepare a place for you . . . that you also may be where I am" (John 14:2–3).

As soon as God has prepared the new earth—full of flowers and colors and mountains and valleys and incredible landscapes—the great city of New Jerusalem will descend from heaven, its brilliant foundations ready to clamp into its preformed 5,600-mile perimeter on the new earth.

At this moment, the seen and the unseen realms will merge. Ephesians 1:9–10 says, "He made known to us the mystery of his will according to his good pleasure, which he purposed in Christ, to be put into effect when the times reach their fulfillment—to bring unity to all things in heaven and on earth under Christ."

Currently there are two realms—the visible and the invisible, the physical and the spiritual. As New Jerusalem descends to the new earth, these two realms will merge into one. The next verses, Revelation 21:3–4, say,

> I heard a loud voice from the throne saying, "Look! God's dwelling place is now among the people, and he will dwell with them. They will be his people, and God himself will be with them and be their God." . . . The old order of things has passed away.

> *God will banish tears, death, mourning, crying, and pain. Those things are gone forever.*

God will banish tears, death, mourning, crying, and pain. Those things are gone forever.

In verse 9, an angel escorts John to one of the high mountains on the new earth so he can have an unfettered view of what happens next. A massive city, sparkling like a diamond and radiating with wondrous light, appears high in the sky and slowly descends to the new earth. John was able to describe it in detail. Verse 11 says,

> *It shone with the glory of God, and its brilliance was like that of a very precious jewel, like a jasper, clear as crystal.*

As we learned earlier, this stone is probably a diamond-like jewel. Can you see this in your mind? An entire colossal city descending to the new earth, sparkling like a jewel. As I've mentioned, I often think of this before falling asleep, seeing in my mind's eye a vast diamond city gliding onto the new earth like, well, a massive spaceship or space city.

Diamonds are the hardest substance known to science. The only thing that can scratch a diamond is another diamond. They are made from carbon but were formed in the far reaches of the hot earth in the days before dinosaurs.[8] They are coughed up by volcanoes, and the heat and pressure transform them into the most beautiful stones on earth. No other gem reflects, refracts, and disperses light so brilliantly as a diamond.

But an entire diamond city?

Could the Lord do that?

Interestingly, in 2004, scientists discovered a planet they believed was composed mostly of carbon and was one-third pure diamond—a diamond of ten billion trillion trillion carats.[9] It orbits a nearby star in the Milky Way, and its official name is 55 Cancri e. Since its discovery, astronomers have decided the planet may not be as carbon-based as first thought, but it started a new line of research. Astronomers now believe there may be many planets made of diamond material. They call these potential finds "diamond planets."[10]

I'm not suggesting such a planet is the city of New Jerusalem. But if God is capable of creating diamonds on our planet and diamond planets in our universe, imagine a city of which He is the designer, architect, and builder! This is Jasper Jerusalem—the Celestial City that sparkles like a diamond in every direction.

Verses 12 and 14 say,

*If God is capable of creating diamonds on our planet and diamond planets in our universe, imagine a city of which He is the designer, architect, and builder!*

> *It had a great, high wall with twelve gates. . . . The wall of the city had twelve foundations.*

The twelve gates are inscribed with the names of the twelve tribes of Israel (God's Old Testament channel of redemption), and the foundations are inscribed with the names of the twelve apostles (representing the church, God's New Testament channel of redemption). This reminds me of the twenty-four elders, which, as I said, may represent the redeemed of all the ages. God's two great channels of redemption are the Jewish nation to produce the Messiah and the church to proclaim the Messiah. There were twelve patriarchs and tribes in Israel and twelve apostles in the church. All twenty-four names are listed on the separate foundation stones and gateways of this city.

Now John was brought even closer, right up to the walls and gates. His tour guide, an angel, had a golden measuring device, and the dimensions measured 1,400 miles in all directions: long, wide, and high. A city this size (about 2 million square miles) is larger than the nation of India (1,240,000 square miles).

The walls are two hundred feet thick, and John took pains to point out that these are literal human measurements (v. 17).

Verse 18 tells us the walls are made of the same diamond-like material that characterizes the entire city, but here it is described as a kind of transparent gold:

*The city [was made] of pure gold, as pure as glass.*

As I imagine this, I simply see a diamond city with a rich tinting of gold. You can study this passage and find your own mental images for it, but God has certainly given us these details so we can hold them in our minds and ponder them with great anticipation.

The foundations of the city are composed of massive jewels, the most beautiful jewels and precious stones ever seen. Each of the twelve gates appears as a giant pearl (vv. 19–21). I take that to mean huge portals of ivory-colored porcelain of some kind, exceedingly beautiful. We'll pass through these broad, wide-open gates every time we come and go from the city.

Revelation 22:14 says we will have the right to the Tree of Life and may go through the gates into the city. In his book *Heaven*, Randy Alcorn wrote,

> Fifteen times in Revelation 21 and 22 the place God and his people will live together is called a city. The repetition of the word and the detailed description of the architecture, walls, streets, and other features of the city suggest that the term *city* isn't merely a figure of speech but a literal geographical location. After all, where do we expect physically resurrected people to live if not in a physical environment?
>
> Everyone knows what a city is—a place with buildings, streets, and residences occupied by people and subject to a common government. Cities have inhabitants, visitors, bustling activity, cultural events, and gatherings involving music, the arts,

education, religion, entertainment, and athletics. If the capital city of the New Earth doesn't have these defining characteristics of a city, it would seem misleading for Scripture to repeatedly call it a city.[11]

Alcorn makes a critical point. Jesus rose physically and bodily from the grave. His body was physically crucified and endured prolonged excruciating pain. He literally died. Three days later at the moment of His resurrection, His body was changed, transformed, glorified, and fitted for eternity. It was ageless. It was imperishable. Yet it was still His own physical self, His literal person in a resurrected and real body. He told His disciples to touch Him, and He invited them to eat with Him.

Since our resurrection bodies will be like His, the clear and certain implication is we'll dwell in a literal geographical location. Physical bodies require a literal place in which to exist.

Next, John has somehow slipped through the gate into the city itself, and he was overwhelmed. The grand boulevard of the city is pure gold, the same gold that has transparency to it (v. 21). It apparently cuts or winds through all fourteen hundred miles, undoubtedly with many cross-streets and intersecting avenues.

In verse 23, he said,

*The city does not need the sun or the moon to shine on it, for the glory of God gives it light, and the Lamb is its lamp.*

John did not say there is no sun or moon to enlighten and grace the new earth. He simply said that in the capital city, the sun and moon are superfluous because the city is always lit up by the radiance of the glory of God. This, again, is literal. Remember when Jesus appeared on the Mount of Transfiguration? His face, indeed His whole body, shone like the sun. Paul described God as One "who alone is immortal and who lives in unapproachable light"

*In the capital city, the sun and moon are superfluous because the city is always lit up by the radiance of the glory of God.*

(1 Timothy 6:16). In Hebrew, this is referred to as the *shekinah* glory of God.[12] In English, we might say "the glory clouds of God."

How can we even see with such blinding resplendence? After all, when the apostle Paul saw Christ on the Damascus Road, he was instantly blinded (Acts 9:8). The wonderful answer is that our bodies will be transformed at the resurrection to be like Christ's resurrection body (Philippians 3:21). They will be imperishable and immortal (1 Corinthians 15:53). Our eyes will be upgraded for eternity.

With these physical bodies, we will need places to live. Jesus indicated that in His Father's house are many dwelling places, and His Father's house seems to refer to heaven—the new heavens and the new earth.

Verses 24–26 say,

*The nations will walk by its light, and the kings of the earth will bring their splendor into it. On no day will its gates ever be shut, for there will be no night there. The glory and honor of the nations will be brought into it.*

Notice the mention of *nations* on the new earth. In terms of our location, we'll not be limited to New Jerusalem, which I imagine will be the capital of the new earth. We will populate the entire city and the entire earth in an organized way. There will be systems and organizational structures, not chaos.

I see no reason why we may not have both a home in the city and another somewhere else on the new earth. Perhaps those who want to travel throughout the universe and see the beauties of the intergalactic cosmos can do so. Our bodies will have properties far beyond those we now possess. We'll be transformed in this new merged world of the physical and the spiritual realms.

We'll also have meaningful activities. Since we're talking about eternity, we'll have endless options and opportunities. I often think I'd like to take up oil painting in heaven, and I'd love to become an accomplished pianist to play the hymns I love and some of the piano jazz I like. Please don't think I'm making light of all this. I believe these verses tell us we'll be creative and productive. There will be trade and commerce, organized nations, and perfect government. Everything God does is organized, and with billions of people and angels populating the new earth, it will be well arranged yet loving and unthreatening.

All in all, our inheritance in heaven will be literal, fabulous, physical, and eternal.

In Revelation 22:1–2, John was taken farther into the capital, to the very center of the city. There he saw the greatest sight in all of time and eternity—the glorious throne of Almighty God, and from beneath it a mighty river flowing as clear as crystal. Just take a moment to imagine it. This is my single favorite scene in all of the Bible.

> *Then the angel showed me the river of the water of life, as clear as crystal, flowing from the throne of God and of the Lamb down the middle of the great street of the city. On each side of the river stood the tree of life.*

I take this to be an orchard of trees of life. Oh, to get a glimpse of this! In the heart of the golden, diamond city is the enormous throne of our glorious God—just as literal and real as the resurrection body of Christ—and gushing like Niagara from the throne are the head-waters of a glorious crystal-clear river flowing alongside the lanes of the golden central boulevard, surrounded by the most beautiful gardens ever designed, filled with trees of life.

As my wife, Katrina, was dying, I made a date with her to stroll along this river.

## Ezekiel's River

The crystal river that gushes from beneath the throne of God is eternal. This is heaven itself. But we get a preview of it from the book of Ezekiel, which describes the Millennial Temple during our Lord's thousand-year reign. Ezekiel's millennial river is a sneak peek at the crystal river of New Jerusalem. He wrote,

> In my vision, the man brought me back to the entrance of the Temple. There I saw a stream flowing east from beneath the door of the Temple. . . . The river was too deep to walk across. It was deep enough to swim in. . . . I was surprised by the sight of many trees growing on both sides of the river. . . . Fruit trees of all kinds will grow along both sides of the river. The leaves of these trees will never turn brown and fall, and there will always be fruit on their branches. There will be a new crop every month, for they are watered by the river flowing from the Temple. (Ezekiel 47:1–12 NLT)

Visualizing Ezekiel's description of the millennial river and its lush parks and riverbanks helps me better imagine the crystal river of New Jerusalem, which will surely refresh the entire new earth.

Verse 3 says,

> *No longer will there be any curse. The throne of God and of the Lamb will be in the city, and his servants will serve him.*

The curse that marred the old creation is nowhere to be seen in the new. And what will we be doing? Serving! As I've indicated, we'll be busy with meaningful activity throughout eternity.

Heaven will involve constant natural music and praise and worship, but it's not going to be like a never-ending church service. We'll have productive activity, wonderful fellowship, and constant access to the throne and to Him who sits on it. We'll have positions of authority and opportunities for humble service.

We'll have endless time for refreshing fellowship with the saints of all the ages, with all the heroes of biblical and Christian history. We'll meet our ancestors who served Christ decades and centuries before we came along. Best of all, most of all, we will literally see the face of our Lord Jesus Christ and interact with Him, fellowship with Him, worship Him, and abide with Him.

Verse 4 says, *They will see His face.*

"Then we will be with the Lord forever" (1 Thessalonians 4:17).

*And they will reign for ever and ever* (Revelation 22:5).

*He who testifies to these things says, "Yes, I am coming soon"* (Revelation 22:20).

Hallelujah!

# The Spirit and the Bride Say, "Come!"

You still have questions, don't you?

So do I.

My son-in-law Joshua reminded me yesterday that only after the first coming of Christ could Bible students fully recognize and assemble all the predictions about it. God gave Israel lots of information—over three hundred specific predictions about Christ's coming to earth and a ton of types and adumbrations. They had enough information to assemble a reasonable view of what would happen. But only in retrospect could they—and can we—put it all together in a way that allows us to see its fullness and perfection.

In the same way, it takes enjoyable years of study to assemble the pieces of the puzzle God has given us about His second coming, and there's great edification in the process. Every prayerful study of biblical prophecy makes us keen for the future, excited about our Lord's return, and zealous to complete the work He's given us on earth.

*Every prayerful study of biblical prophecy makes us keen for the future, excited about our Lord's return, and zealous to complete the work He's given us on earth.*

It's a brilliant way of teaching us. The Lord's predictive truths are woven throughout His Word, so wherever we are reading in the Bible, we're not far from one.

Each one builds "the hope to which he has called you, the riches of his glorious inheritance in his holy people" (Ephesians 1:18). The apostle Peter, referring to the Old Testament prophets who predicted the comings of Christ, said, "The prophets, who spoke of the grace that was to come to you, searched intently and with the greatest care, trying to find out the time and circumstances to which the Spirit of Christ in them was pointing when he predicted the sufferings of the Messiah and the glories that would follow. . . . Even angels long to look into these things" (1 Peter 1:10–12).

Like the Bible students of old, we're to search the Scriptures intently and with greatest care, trying to find out the circumstances related to the return of Christ. That's what I've tried to do in this book. I may not have every detail figured out yet. Well, I definitely do not. But I do believe the general outlines are clear—just as clear as the outline of the book of Revelation.

Right now, we're living Revelation 2–3, in the days of the church, and we must keep ourselves pure, strong, healthy, and gospel-centered.

At some point, perhaps soon, a crisis on earth will trigger a fresh global response from the governments of the world, and current events will take on an ominous tone.

Meanwhile in heaven, a worship service at the throne of God (Revelation 4–5) will serve as a prelude to Christ's launching a seven-year period of worldwide stress for the sake of evangelism and judgment. Fifty events, as I've listed them from the pages of Revelation, will unfold, one after the other.

For forty-two months, while Israel is under the protection of a peace treaty, the world will convulse with major disasters and geopolitical agitation, and God will begin a series of judgments (the seals and the trumpets) that will cause multitudes of people to seek Him and be saved through faith in Christ (Revelation 6–11).

In the middle of these seven years, the global leader will be assassinated and resurrected (or appear to be so) and possessed by the devil. This tyrant will demand to be worshiped by the Jewish people in their temple, and they will refuse (Revelation 12–13).

That will unleash a time of distress never before equaled in history as the armies of the world unite with the Antichrist's confederacy and march toward Israel to destroy the Jewish people. God will pour out seven bowls of wrath as His enemies converge at Armageddon. Israel will be ravaged, Jerusalem breached (Revelation 14–18).

At that moment when all seems lost and the world is engulfed in total chaos, Jesus Christ will return, put a swift end to the battle, and save His people Israel, both spiritually and politically (Revelation 19). He will reign on earth a thousand years from Israel's capital, Jerusalem. At the end of this period, the unsaved dead will rise to be judged and condemned (Revelation 20).

And finally, at last, Jesus will be with His people forever in the new heaven, the new earth, and the city of New Jerusalem, where righteousness dwells—and so shall we be with the Lord forever (Revelation 21–22).

Are you ready for these events? Is your family? Are your loved ones?

The final invitation in the Bible says,

*The Spirit and the bride say, "Come!" And let the one who hears say, "Come!" Let the one who is thirsty come; and let the one who wishes take the free gift of the water of life.* (Revelation 22:17)

I encourage you with all my heart to come to Jesus today. Take His free gift of eternal blessings and an everlasting inheritance. In prayer, confess your sins and be willing to turn from all that's evil and unhealthy in your life by God's grace and with His strength. Acknowledge Jesus Christ as your living Savior, and give your life to Him today.

And don't be afraid of the world tomorrow. God's grace is aggressive, available, and immeasurable. His plans are outlined in His Word. His love is everlasting, and His truth endures forever. He loves you more than you know, and He is eager to be your Savior and your Sovereign forever.

We have so much ahead of us—an inheritance unending, a life everlasting!

Don't look around you and be distressed. Look ahead and be blessed!

Hallelujah!

Maranatha!

*He who testifies to these things says, "Yes, I am coming soon."*
*Amen. Come, Lord Jesus.*
*The grace of the Lord Jesus be with God's people. Amen.*

REVELATION 22:20–21

# The Five Views of Revelation

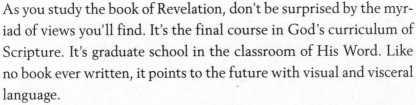

As you study the book of Revelation, don't be surprised by the myriad of views you'll find. It's the final course in God's curriculum of Scripture. It's graduate school in the classroom of His Word. Like no book ever written, it points to the future with visual and visceral language.

In *The 50 Final Events in World History*, I've sought to make the flow of material in Revelation simple enough for a middle schooler or a beginning Bible student. With the right approach, Revelation loses some of its perplexity but none of its marvel and mystery. I've read some complicated explanations of Revelation, packed with enigmatic insights from brilliant scholars. But I often find myself thinking, *If this book is written for millions of everyday, sincere students of the Bible, isn't it best to embrace the most natural reading?*

The most natural reading, it seems to me, simply takes each verse in turn, each scene as it comes, and each chapter, one after another, and follows the flow of events from the opening scene in heaven in Revelation 4–5 to our eternal home in heaven in Revelation 21–22. The intervening chapters—Revelation 8–20—tell us what will happen in stages.

Revelation is a book for every believer. It may be the deep end of the pool, but those who study it develop a natural buoyancy.

Those who read it are blessed. In its twenty-two chapters Jesus gives us a personal tour of the events related to His return to earth. He explains the various events, each one succeeding the next, so we can

1. know that evil will be judged and removed from the universe;
2. anticipate our eternal future;
3. be strong, faithful, and holy in our daily lives as we await our glorious hope;
4. be comforted in times of loss; and
5. be confident in the unshakable power of Christ and in the eternal reign of our Almighty God.

The graphic visions in Revelation convey the sensational nature of the events it describes. It's meant to be breathtaking. But not unintelligible.

## Futurist

The approach I take to all this is called *futurist*. In other words, I believe this book is full of prophecies about the future. Most of the material—especially chapter 4 and onward—is about the world tomorrow. How wonderfully does our loving Lord do this for His children! He gives us what He knows we need: only as much information as we can absorb about the glorious hope awaiting us.

To me, Revelation is a chronological tour of the years preceding the return of Christ. Despite all its symbols and visuals, the 404 verses of Revelation are stepping-stones into the future, and what you see is what you get. One thing happens after another, and at the end of the process we're ushered into heaven.

There are variations of opinion among futurists regarding how some of the events in Revelation align. Nevertheless, they believe the material is a prophetic picture of the events leading powerfully to the return of Christ.

## Preterists

Not everyone agrees with futurism. Some interpreters adopt the *preterist* approach. The term comes from the Latin word *praeter,* a term meaning "the past." Preterists believe most of the events described in Revelation occurred in the first century, not long after John wrote the book. After all, the book begins by saying, *The revelation from Jesus Christ, which God gave him to show his servants what must soon take place* (Revelation 1:1). Notice the word *soon.* Jesus indicated that the prophecies He gave about His return would be fulfilled within a generation (Matthew 24:34), and preterists interpret that quite literally.

Preterists believe Jesus and John were describing events that were about to occur in the first century—events related to the Roman Empire, the destruction of Jerusalem and Judea in AD 70, and the persecution of Christians. That means the book of Revelation must have been written in the 60s, before the fall of Jerusalem in AD 70. Many preterists interpret the Beast out of the Sea to be Emperor Nero, and others even say it refers to the persecuting Jewish opponents of the early church.

A variation of this view suggests the book is essentially a prediction of the fall of the Roman Empire, which occurred in the fifth century. In any event, for preterists, what John wrote has already taken place, except perhaps for the return of Christ and the eternal state.

Dr. R. C. Sproul, whom I admire very much, adhered to the preterist view, and Hank Hanegraaff appears to embrace a form of this view.

Interestingly, this view developed during the counter-Reformation among Catholics who were tired of their papal system being called the scarlet beast out of the sea and the Antichrist by the Reformers, who held a view we'll look at next—historicism.

# Historicists

*Historicism* was popular during the days of the Reformation but has fewer adherents today. According to historicism, the chapters of Revelation predict a series of time periods between John's day and the return of Christ. In other words, the different scenes represent different stages in the history of Western Europe—the early Christian era, the legalization of Christianity in the 300s, the Dark Ages, the rise of the papacy, the Reformation, and so forth. This view was popular from the days of Martin Luther to the time of Charles Spurgeon, although every generation recalculated the way the pieces fit together. Martin Luther thought the beast out of the sea—the Antichrist—was the Roman papal system.

# Idealists

The *idealist* view interprets the various scenes in Revelation as general symbols of the ongoing conflict between good and evil, between the forces of God and the forces of Satan, with no specific historical or prophetic events linked to them. It's like a kaleidoscope of ever-changing forms and patterns that convey in general terms the struggles leading to the return of Christ. According to idealists, Revelation is full of spiritual lessons but contains little specific prophecy. The theologian Karl Barth was an idealist.

# Eclectics

More recently, some commentators have borrowed elements of all the above systems (especially the idealist theory) and collected them into a view known as *eclecticism*. George Ladd and Greg K. Beale are advocates of this view. The scenes in Revelation recapitulate over and over the struggle between good and evil, leading up to the final and complete victory of Christ over Satan. I'm not an eclectic, but I do appreciate Beale's understanding of the pervasive presence of Old Testament references in the pages of Revelation and his awareness of the historical-cultural context of its human author and early readers.

It's a fascinating thing to consider: Though no single Old Testament verse is quoted verbatim in Revelation, there are phrases and pictures from the Old Testament in 278 of its 404 verses. John's writing also demonstrates his familiarity with Second Temple Jewish literature, especially the apocalyptic writings composed between 200 BC and his own day.

That brings up two questions.

### Question 1: Did John simply repurpose Old Testament writings?

How do we explain the pervasive nature of Old Testament material in Revelation, although there is not a single Old Testament quotation?

Well, John certainly had a masterful grasp on the Old Testament, but that doesn't mean he simply fabricated his book from his knowledge of the Hebrew Scriptures. The book of Revelation is not a matter of John taking various images in the Old Testament and hammering them into a new book. Were that true, we would see verbatim quotations.

I think it's better to put it like this: The things John saw were consistent with what Ezekiel and Daniel saw. John was experiencing visions that corresponded with Old Testament truth. When he saw the throne of God, it was the same throne Moses, Isaiah, Ezekiel, and Daniel had glimpsed. John wasn't simply borrowing Old Testament language; he was learning truth from the same One who had inspired the Old Testament.

The Lord didn't tell John, "Take a large number of Old Testament passages and put them in a new form." He said, *Write on a scroll what you see* (Revelation 1:11). *Write, therefore, what you have seen* (Revelation 1:19). John said, *Then I heard a voice from heaven say, "Write this . . ."* (Revelation 14:13).

Revelation 21:5 says, *He who was seated on the throne said, "I am making everything new!" Then he said, "Write this down, for these words are trustworthy and true."*

Though John knew well the Old Testament and apocryphal Second Temple writings, he wasn't simply repurposing the material. He was writing new material, given to him by the same God who had earlier spoken to Abraham, David, Isaiah, Ezekiel, Daniel, Zechariah, and, yes, Jesus.

The apostle John had a lifetime of immersion into the Old Testament and the intertestamental writings, and that impacted his vocabulary and writing style. But the visions that came to him on the rugged rock of Patmos were fresh, vivid, detailed, and true. What he saw and wrote corresponded perfectly with the rest of Scripture and serves as the capstone of God's revealed Truth.

**Question 2: What comfort would Revelation be to John's readers?**

Critics of futurism sometimes ask another question: If the events described in Revelation were originally addressed to first-century readers about events that wouldn't occur for at least two thousand years, what immediate comfort would it give them?

Would John really say, "Well, don't worry. God will solve all this in a few millennia"?

But remember this: The early predictions of our Lord's first coming were given two thousand years before He showed up in Bethlehem. The seeds of Messianic prophecy were sown in Genesis 12 in the promises God gave Abraham. The long centuries between Abraham and Jesus were packed with additional prophecies about the life and ministry of the Messiah. Bible students of every age "searched intently and with the greatest care, trying to find out the time and circumstances to which the Spirit of Christ in them was pointing when he predicted the sufferings of the Messiah and the glories that would follow" (1 Peter 1:10–11).

There was therapy in the search, and there still is!

Nothing compares with knowing that God has a plan for world history and seeking to discern it within the pages of His Book. Though the ages twist and turn—sometimes like a river and sometimes like a serpent—they are flowing inexorably toward the return of Christ. The more we study this in Scripture, the more we "long for his appearing" (2 Timothy 4:8). The more we long for His appearing, the happier and healthier we'll be.

Jesus told His disciples, "I will come back and take you to be with me so that you also may be where I am" (John 14:3). He spoke those words two thousand years ago, but they have comforted every generation.

The apostle Paul told the persecuted Thessalonians, "God is just: He will pay back trouble for those who trouble you and give relief to you who are troubled, and to us as well. This will happen when the Lord Jesus is revealed from heaven in blazing fire with his powerful angels" (2 Thessalonians 1:6–7). He wrote those words two thousand years ago; they comforted the Thessalonians and have strengthened every subsequent age.

Long ago the apostle Peter said, "Do not forget this one thing, dear friends: With the Lord a day is like a thousand years, and a thousand years are like a day. The Lord is not slow in keeping his promise, as some understand slowness. . . . But the day of the Lord will come like a thief. The heavens will disappear with a roar; the elements will be destroyed by fire, and the earth and everything done in it will be laid bare" (2 Peter 3:8–10).

Then he asked, "Since everything will be destroyed in this way, what kind of people ought you to be? You ought to live holy and godly lives as you look forward to the day of God and speed its coming" (vv. 11–12).

Because God has a plan for history . . . because Jesus is coming . . .

because heaven is real, we have something to anticipate. We look forward to it every day. And that glorious hope motivates us to live with greater hope and holiness and to share the message with others. We walk and work in the light of His impending return.

> Let our songs abound
> And every tear be dry,
> We're marching through Emmanuel's ground
> To fairer worlds on high.

> Isaac Watts

# Revelation on a Napkin

My thesis in *The 50 Final Events in World History* is that Revelation is understandable, that God wants us to anticipate the reality of His coming victory and the broad outlines of earth's final days and the Glory to follow. More than a few times, I've pulled out an ink pen and sketched the outline of Revelation on a napkin while meeting someone for coffee. You can do the same!

First, I draw a rectangle and label it *REV.*

*REV*

Next, I draw three vertical lines like this:

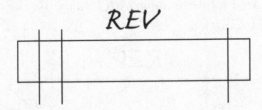

I use abbreviations to designate these as introduction (I), seven churches (7 and a sketch of a church building), and heaven (H). I also add the chapter numbers below.

I explain that the first chapter of Revelation is the book's introduction, giving its author, recipients, purpose, and opening vision—the enthroned Christ, who appeared to John. The next two chapters are individual messages to seven churches, and we can learn how to follow Christ better by the counsel they contain. The last two chapters describe our heavenly home.

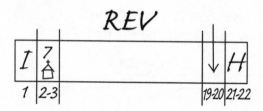

I then draw another line with an added arrow and explain that chapters 19–20 describe the second coming of Christ and what He'll do when He returns.

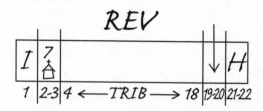

That leaves the middle part of the book—chapters 4–18. These chapters describe seven years of tribulation, when evil is judged and earth is prepared for its reunion with Jesus. I use the abbreviation *TRIB* for the tribulation.

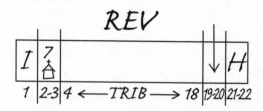

Using a dotted line, I box off chapters 4–5, saying those chapters describe the scene at the throne of God at the beginning of the tribulation. I use a *T* for throne, with a circle around it, because the throne was encircled by the heavenly host.

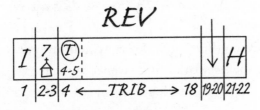

Now we have chapters 6–18, which describe what will happen on earth during these seven years. In the middle of the remaining space I draw a circle and say that is the midpoint in the tribulation.

The rest is easy. Chapters 6–11 describe the first half of the

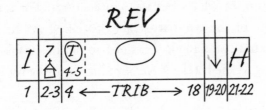

tribulation, which is marked by the opening of the seven seals and the blowing of seven trumpets, all representing judgments that will fall on the earth. I put two sevens in this space and indicate this is chapters 6–11.

The middle of the tribulation is described in chapters 12–13. And the last half of the tribulation is in chapters 14–18, which describe the final judgments—seven bowls of wrath poured out on the earth. It ends with the battle of Armageddon, which I illustrate using a bolt of lightning.

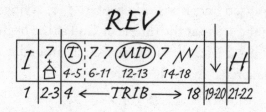

Having drawn this sketch, I review it all simply.

The book of Revelation has twenty-two chapters. The first is introductory. The next two are messages to the churches of the last days.

The unfolding events of the tribulation begin with the throne scene in chapters 4–5. The events on earth will unfold over seven years.

The first three and a half years will be marked by seven seals and seven trumpets, described in chapters 6–11. The terrible events of the middle of the tribulation are described in chapters 12–13, and the last three and a half years of tribulation unfold in chapters 14–18, ending in the battle of Armageddon and the return of Christ in chapters 19–20.

The final two chapters tell us of God's perfect eternal kingdom, where we will see Jesus, serve Him, and be with His people forever.

I often tell the person, "While the details and images of Revelation may seem overwhelming, the overall structure and message of the book is as simple as saying, 'God is working now in His church, and one day soon a cataclysm of some sort will trigger the final seven years of history preceding His return.'

"Here is the outline of Revelation. By understanding this, your further study of the details will make more sense. Don't be afraid of Revelation. It's as exciting as the Lord's return and will help prepare us for that glorious day."

# Genesis, Revelation, and the Circle of Scripture

When we compare the first three chapters of the Bible with the last three, we find a story that comes full circle. The issues and dilemmas raised in Genesis 1–3 are addressed and perfectly resolved in Revelation 20–22.

- In Genesis 1:1, God created the heavens and the earth. In Revelation 21:1, He created the *new* heavens and earth.
- In Genesis 2, God created Paradise—the garden of Eden—on earth for His people. In Revelation 21, a new paradise—the New Jerusalem—dominates the earth.
- In Genesis 3, Adam and Eve heard the Lord's voice in the cool of the day. In Revelation 22, we'll see His face and we'll fellowship with Him forever.
- In Genesis 2, the Tree of Life sat in the middle of the garden. In Revelation 22, we find the same tree in the middle of God's city.
- In the garden of Eden, four rivers flowed through the land. In Revelation 22, the river of the water of life irrigates New Jerusalem.

- Genesis 2:12 says the gold of Eden was good. In Revelation 21–22, we glimpse a city with streets of gold.
- Genesis 2:15 says God placed Adam and Eve in the garden of Eden to tend it. Revelation 22:3 says His servants will be busy serving Him forever.
- Death came onto humanity in Genesis 3. At the end of Revelation, death is abolished forever and with it all tears and suffering.
- Pain is introduced in Genesis 3:16. It is banished in Revelation 21:4.
- The devil was absent in the first two chapters of the Bible, showing up in Genesis 3. In Revelation 19, he is thrown into the lake of fire and is wonderfully absent from the last two chapters of the Bible.
- In Genesis 3:17, the ground was cursed because of sin. Revelation 22:3 says there will be no more curse.
- The gates of Eden were shut to humanity in Genesis 3:23–24. But the gates of God's city to come will never be shut by day or night (Revelation 21:25).
- The first three chapters of the Bible tell us the beginning of God's story for the world. It is completed perfectly in the last three chapters.

When we open the Bible, we discover a sovereign God creating a universe as home for the people He was about to make in His own image. He placed them in an environment of paradise, but Satan came and spoiled the scene.

Sixty-six books come and go, telling the story of God's redemptive plan through one Savior, Christ Jesus.

At the end of the Bible, chaos is judged, Satan is banished, death is destroyed, the curse is lifted, and Paradise is better than ever—eternal, glorified, united, the seen and unseen realms joined under one head, Christ Jesus.

Only a Master Author could have written so wonderful a Book and given us a story that comes full circle and truly ends happily ever after.

Maranatha! Even so, come, Lord Jesus!

# Will We Know One
# Another in Heaven?

The descriptions in Revelation 21–22 of the new heavens, new earth, and new Jerusalem are literal—or they are images of an even more literal reality—and how wonderful is that? We will literally, physically, and bodily be with the Godhead, the godly personalities of the invisible realm, the saints of all the ages, and one another for eternity. Wouldn't it be a shame if we never recognized anyone? Is it possible we'll be total strangers in paradise forever, that we'll have everlasting amnesia?

No. It isn't remotely possible—yet we sometimes wonder if we'll know each other in heaven. It's an emotive question. Our relationships on earth mean more to us than anything else. I loved my dad and mom; I love my sister and her family; I miss my wife, and I cherish daughters, their husbands, and all their children. These relationships are more valuable to me than any other single thing in this world apart from my relationship with Christ. I never want to lose these bonds of love. It doesn't matter if I lose everything else on earth, I don't want to lose those dearest to me. I want to be where they are, and I want them to be where I am.

Jesus felt the same way. In the upper room on the eve of His crucifixion, Jesus told the disciples, "If I go and prepare a place for you, I will come back and take you to be with me that you also may be where I am" (John 14:3).

He wanted His friends to be with Him, near Him, fellowshipping with Him forever. A couple of hours later, Jesus prayed an unutterably deep prayer just before His arrest. "Father," He said, "I want those you have given me to be with me where I am" (John 17:24).

Jesus Himself—God of very God—wanted His friends and family to be with Him in eternity, where He was, so He could enjoy their fellowship and love. He feels as we do about our dearest ones. These passages in John 14 and 17 clearly imply that one of the greatest joys of heaven will be our everlasting reunion with those we love.

While the Bible doesn't give us a verse saying, "You will know each other in heaven," it treats this reality like an obvious truth, simply assuming this is the case. There are a number of passages that make this assumption reasonable and clear.

## John 20:19–23

The resurrection of Jesus Christ gives us our first glimpse in Scripture of what the glorified resurrection body will be like. John 20:19–20 says, "On the evening of that first day of the week, when the disciples were together, with the doors locked for fear of the Jewish leaders, Jesus came and stood among them and said, 'Peace be with you!' After he said this, he showed them his hands and side. The disciples were overjoyed when they saw the Lord."

When Jesus rose from the tomb, He had the same identity and the same appearance He had prior to His death. The disciples recognized Him. They recognized His face and His features, they recognized His hands with the nail prints, and He even showed them His side. They recognized Him by the scar left from the Roman spear. He knew them after His resurrection, and they knew Him, though His body was now imperishable.

I've long believed that our resurrection bodies will have the appearance of our being in our early thirties. Jesus was about thirty-three when He rose from the dead, and Philippians 3:21 says He will "transform our lowly bodies so that they will be like his glorious body." Whatever our apparent age, we will be physically, mentally, and emotionally mature, and we will be recognizable as ourselves. The essence of our identity will not be lost through the process of rapture or resurrection. Our faults and failures will be gone, but I will still be me, and you will still be you—in the fullness of the perfection of Christ.

## 1 Corinthians 13:12

Another clue comes from 1 Corinthians 13. In the first several verses, the apostle Paul commended the virtues of love, and he ended the chapter by talking about its permanence. Love will continue after we die. Faith will not be needed in heaven, and our hope will be fulfilled. But love will continue. Our relationships with those we love will go right on, and, in fact, be far better.

"Now we see only a reflection as in a mirror; then we shall see face to face. Now I know in part; then I shall know fully, even as I am fully known" (1 Corinthians 13:12).

In other words, "I know Jesus Christ now, but one day I'll know Him better; I'll see Him fully and I will know Him just as He knows me." The implication is that we'll also know each other better and love each other more fully in the future than we do now.

Right now, even the best of human relationships are imperfect. One day those of us who know Christ Jesus our Lord will see His face, reflect His love, and know one another even as we ourselves are known.

# 1 Thessalonians 4

Another helpful passage is in 1 Thessalonians. The Christians in Thessalonica were still learning the rudiments of Christian theology. They had questions about what happens when we die. Paul wrote,

> Brothers and sisters, we do not want you to be uninformed about those who sleep in death, so that you do not grieve like the rest of mankind, who have no hope. For we believe that Jesus died and rose again, and so we believe that God will bring with Jesus those who have fallen asleep in him. According to the Lord's word, we tell you that we who are still alive, who are left until the coming of the Lord, will certainly not precede those who have fallen asleep. For the Lord himself will come down from heaven, with a loud command, with the voice of the archangel and with the trumpet call of God, and the dead in Christ will rise first. After that, we who are still alive and are left will be caught up together with them in the clouds to meet the Lord in the air. And so we will be with the Lord forever. Therefore encourage one another with these words. (1 Thessalonians 4:13–18)

The basis of Paul's encouragement and comfort is that we'll be together with those we love and with the Lord forever in heaven. Our fellowship with our Christian loved ones goes right on! We'll pick up where we left off, and we will know even as we are known. We will recognize Him and others, even as they recognize us.

There's no capping the encouragement this gives me!

# 2 Corinthians 4:13–14

In a similar vein, in 2 Corinthians 4:14, Paul wrote, "We know that the one who raised the Lord Jesus from the dead will also raise us with Jesus and present us with you in His presence."

Paul *knew* something. He didn't hope, think, speculate, or wish. He *knew* his body would be resurrected and he would be reunited with his Corinthian friends in the presence of the Lord. That gave him vast encouragement, and he repeated the same idea elsewhere in his letters to his friends and to other churches he established. For example, he called the Thessalonians "the crown in which we will glory in the presence of the Lord Jesus when he comes" (1 Thessalonians 2:19).

He fully anticipated an eternal friendship with those he had won to Christ.

# Luke 16:22–31

In Luke 16, Jesus told about a neighborhood beggar who died and went to heaven. But Jesus didn't use the word *heaven*. He used the phrase *Abraham's side*, saying, "The time came when the beggar died and the angels carried him to Abraham's side." The passage goes on to talk about "Abraham . . . with Lazarus by his side" (Luke 16:22–23).

In other words, a dirty but God-trusting Middle Eastern beggar went to heaven and found himself walking down the street side by side with Abraham, the greatest figure of the Old Testament. The whole story is based on the premise that we will know one another in heaven. Though their earthly timelines had been separated by two thousand years, Abraham and the beggar knew one another and fellowshipped together.

I don't know if they knew one another instinctively or if they were introduced to each other. I'm curious about this. When I get to heaven, will I instinctively know my grandfather, who was a mountain preacher and died long before I was born? Or will he come up to me and say, "On earth, I was your grandfather"?

I don't know, but I'm looking forward to knowing him, along with Abraham, the beggar of Luke 16, and all the other heroes of the faith. One small hint that our knowledge may be instinctive comes from the next passage.

## Matthew 17:1-8

The transfiguration of Christ was the moment when Peter, James, and John caught a glimpse of the intrinsic, eternal glory of their Savior. Matthew 17:1–4 says, "After six days Jesus took with him Peter, James, and John the brother of James, and led them up a high mountain by themselves. There He was transfigured before them. His face shone like the sun, and His clothes became as white as the light."

When Jesus came to earth, He left His throne and its eternal glory. He temporarily relinquished His splendor and some of His divine prerogatives. He entered humanity as a baby in a manger. But on this occasion during His earthly life, He was momentarily enveloped with a flash of His original and eternal glory.

How amazing that two Old Testament heroes joined Him! Moses, Elijah, and Jesus all belonged to different epochs of human history. Moses dates to about 1400 BC, Elijah lived in the 800s BC, and Jesus lived in the first century AD.

Here we have three men whose earthly lives were separated by fourteen hundred years, and yet they all knew each other. They were standing there physically, fellowshipping and talking together. They were known by their same names, but they were glorified, energized, wrapped in light.

This is a sneak peek of heaven!

So, yes, we'll recognize our loved ones in heaven. As someone once put it, we'll certainly not be greater fools in heaven than we are on earth. If we know one another now, we'll certainly know one another in the soon-to-be.

Several years ago, I conducted a worship service at a retirement home. An elderly woman pulled me aside and said she and her husband had been married over sixty years. During their final years together, they used my book *Then Sings My Soul* for their morning devotions. This book tells the story behind our classic hymns. Every morning the couple read the story about a hymn and sang the song. One morning they came to a song popular in bygone days. Written by Charles Gabriel, it was commonly called "The Glory Song." Some of the hymn's words are:

> When all my labors and trials are o'er
> > And I am safe on that beautiful shore,
> > Just to be near the sweet Lord I adore
> > Will thro' the ages be glory for me.

The husband read that song and the story about it, and he said to his wife, "That will be glory for me. I'm ready to go right now."

"But what about me?" she asked.

"Oh," he said, "you have a lot of people to look after you. When I get to heaven, that will be glory for me."

That very day, he went home to heaven. The memory of that final conversation was so sweet and comforting to the woman that she wanted to tell me about it. And she especially delighted, as I do, in the third verse of this great song, which summarizes the spirit of this article:

> Friends will be there I have loved long ago,
> > Joy like a river around me will flow;
> > Yet just a smile from my Savior I know,
> > Will through the ages be glory for me.

# Antiochus IV Epiphanes

## *The Biblical Prototype of the Antichrist*

Is there any way of knowing what the Antichrist will be like?

Yes, we have a historical preview.

In the Old Testament, we often run across people, objects, or events that serve as divine previews of future personalities or episodes. We call these *types* based on verses like Romans 5:14, which calls Adam "a type of Him who was to come" (NKJV), referring to Jesus. In other words, the old Adam was an understated preview of the new Adam—the Lord Jesus. There are parallels between the two.

In engineering, we call these prototypes. In architecture, we call them models. In sewing, we call them patterns.

Types are concrete prophecies, as opposed to verbal prophecies. The book of Hebrews, for example, explains how the high priesthood and tabernacle were pictures of the person and ministry of Christ, our great high priest. According to 1 Corinthians 5:7, the Passover lamb was a prototype of the Lamb of God, who takes away the sin of the world. Jesus said the serpent on the pole in Numbers 21 was a symbol of His crucifixion (John 3:14).

We have many types of Christ in the Old Testament, but did you know we also have types of the Antichrist? Without question, the most prominent example of the latter is Antiochus IV Epiphanes.

Several times in his book, Daniel predicted a coming tyrant in history who would serve as a harbinger for the Antichrist. I want to show you Daniel's prophecies, how they were fulfilled in a character named Antiochus IV Epiphanes, and how they ultimately point to the Antichrist.

## Daniel's Predictions

In the eighth chapter of his book, the prophet and statesman Daniel had a terrifying vision. He saw a ram with two horns raging around furiously. Then a goat with one prominent horn flew across the earth and attacked the ram. The ram perished and the goat grew larger, but at the prime of its strength its horn was broken off. Four smaller horns grew from the spot, pointing in different directions.

One of the four horns grew in power and was pointed toward Israel, the "Beautiful Land." Daniel 8:9–12 says about it,

> Out of one of them came another horn, which started small but grew in power to the south and to the east and toward the Beautiful Land. It grew until it reached the host of the heavens, and it threw some of the starry host down to the earth and trampled on them. It set itself up to be as great as the commander of the army of the Lord; it took away the daily sacrifice from the Lord, and his sanctuary was thrown down. Because of rebellion, the Lord's people and the daily sacrifice were given over to it. It prospered in everything it did, and truth was thrown to the ground.

The meaning of all this is given in verses 20–22: "The two-horned ram that you saw represents the kings of Media and Persia [the Persian Empire]. The shaggy goat is the king of Greece [the Greek Empire], and the large horn between its eyes is the first king [Alexander the Great]. The four horns that replaced the one that was broken off represent four kingdoms that will emerge from his nation but will not have the same power."

All of this unfolded in history exactly as Daniel had predicted. The Persian Empire (the Medes and the Persians, the two-horned ram) was defeated by the Greek Empire of Alexander the Great, who came racing across the world, conquering everything in sight. But at age thirty-two, he died in Babylon. His empire was divided among his four generals, leading to decades of brutal regional conflict.

One of those generals, Seleucus I Nicator, founded the Seleucid dynasty, which controlled much of Asia Minor, Syria, Babylon, and Persia. When he was assassinated in 281 BC, his son took over. He was succeeded in turn by his son, Antiochus I. Twenty years later, he was followed by his son, Antiochus II Theos, who married two women. When Antiochus II died suddenly in 246 BC (probably poisoned by his first wife), a civil war ensued between the two women and their heirs. The region was roiled in conflict for decades, but in 222 BC, Antiochus III the Great gained control of the Seleucid Empire at age eighteen. He died on July 3, 187 BC. His son was Antiochus IV Epiphanes—the little horn of Daniel 8, the eighth ruler of the Seleucid Empire. He came to power about 170 BC.

Daniel predicted all this, not only in chapter 8 of his book but also in chapter 11, which adds more details: "Then a mighty king will arise [Alexander the Great], who will rule with great power and do as he pleases. After he has arisen, his empire will be broken up and parceled out toward the four winds of heaven" (v. 4).

There follows a complicated set of prophecies about the conflicts between Syria and Egypt, but beginning in verse 29 we have another clear prediction of Antiochus IV, including the remarkable prophecy that he will try to invade Egypt but be interdicted by Rome:

At the appointed time he [Antiochus] will invade the South [Egypt] again, but this time the outcome will be different. Ships of the western coastlines [Rome] will oppose him, and he will lose heart. Then he will turn back and vent his fury against the holy covenant [Israel]. . . . His armed forces will desecrate the temple fortress and will abolish the daily sacrifice. Then he will set up the abomination that causes desolation. With flattery he will corrupt those who have violated the covenant, but the people who know their God will firmly resist him. (11:29–32)

## The Past Fulfillment of Daniel's Predictions

The precision of Daniel's predictions are breathtaking in the light of intertestamental history. What Daniel wrote came true to the last letter.

Antiochus IV occupied the throne in the Syrian capital of Antioch (ironically, this is the city that later sent forth the first church-sponsored missionaries in Acts 13). The city was laid out on a grid pattern like that of Alexandria and became home to hundreds of thousands of people. Antioch included a fabulous palace, a theater, gardens, and marvelous Greek buildings of all kinds. It became one of the greatest cities on earth.

Antiochus pretended to be a man of the people, and we're told he sometimes showed up in the public bathhouses where he mingled with the common people, in local booths and workshops where he admired the craftsmanship of artisans, and even in private homes. He sometimes tossed money into the crowds. At banquets, he occasionally got up and danced naked with the entertainers. Other times, he mingled with the masses in disguise to see what was being said in daily conversation.

Despite his genial and outgoing personality, Antiochus had a dark side, as black as midnight. His self-appointed title, Epiphanes, meant "God Manifest." Behind his back he was called Epimames, which meant "the Madman." Fearing the rising Roman threat from the West, Antiochus felt he could strengthen his position by annexing Egypt. He wanted to impose Greek (Hellenistic) culture on everything from Babylon to Egypt.

The little province of Judea and its capital of Jerusalem sat in the middle of Antiochus's projected empire. He determined to turn the Jewish state into a Hellenistic province, strip it of its Jewish culture, and make it thoroughly Greek. He began by replacing the Jewish high priest with one sympathetic to his aims—Joshua, who immediately changed his name to Jason. The new high priest worked to implement Antiochus's plan. Building projects turned Jerusalem into a miniature model of Antioch, complete with a Greek gymnasium where the athletes competed nude. Statutes and temples appeared to Syrian gods. Antiochus raided the temple treasury to fund his military campaign to conquer Egypt.

Some of the Jews, beguiled by Antiochus and his visions, went along with him. But as you might expect, many Jews—largely descendants of the remnant that had returned under Zerubbabel, Ezra, and Nehemiah—revolted. This created civil conflict within Israel.

Meanwhile, Antiochus made his way to Egypt, where his ambitions ran headlong into the rising Roman army. Some accounts say the Roman envoy, Popilius, drew a circle in the sand around Antiochus and demanded he surrender his military campaign before stepping out of the circle.

Stymied in Egypt, Antiochus was humiliated as he returned to Syria by way of Jerusalem. In a blinding rage he slaughtered thousands of people. That led to more rebellion, and Antiochus simply outlawed Judaism. He forbade the Mosaic diet and the study of the Torah. He banned the circumcision of Jewish boys. There was great mourning throughout Israel. It's believed that eighty thousand Jews were killed.

Antiochus ordered a statue of Zeus to be placed in the temple.

This is the famous abomination that caused desolation, a foreshadowing of the midtribulation event that Jesus, Paul, and John warned about. Antiochus had swine sacrificed on the altar. He turned the holy temple into a Greek fortress. His most horrific and almost unspeakable atrocity was the killing of circumcised Jewish baby boys. Syrian soldiers would kill them before their mothers, then crucify the women with their dead babies around their necks as they suffered on the crosses. When something this inhuman occurs, there's a force of supernatural evil behind it.

This history is recounted in several sources, including the intertestamental book of 1 Maccabees, where we read,

> Innocent people were murdered around the altar; the Holy place was defiled by murderers. The people of Jerusalem fled in fear, and the city became a colony of foreigners. . . . Her Temple was as empty as a wilderness, her festivals were turned into days of mourning, her Sabbath joy into shame. . . .
>
> The king also sent messengers with a decree to Jerusalem and all the towns of Judea, ordering the people to follow customs that were foreign to the country. He ordered them not to offer burnt offerings, grain offerings, or wine offerings in the Temple, and commanded them to treat Sabbaths and festivals as ordinary workdays. They were even ordered to defile the Temple and the holy things in it. They were commanded to build pagan altars, temples, and shrines, and to sacrifice pigs and other unclean animals there. They were forbidden to circumcise their sons and were required to make themselves ritually unclean in every way they could, so that they would forget the Law which the Lord had given through Moses and would disobey all its commands. The penalty for disobeying the king's decree was death.
>
> The king . . . also appointed officials to supervise the people and commanded each town in Judea to offer pagan sacrifices. . . .
>
> On the fifteenth day of the month Kislev in the year 145,

King Antiochus set up The Awful Horror on the altar of the Temple, and pagan altars were built in the towns around Judea. Pagan sacrifices were offered in front of houses and in the streets. Any books of the Law which were found were torn up and burned, and everyone who was caught with a copy of the sacred books or who obeyed the Law was put to death. . . .

Mothers who had allowed their babies to be circumcised were put to death in accordance with the king's decree. Their babies were hung around their necks. (GNT)

The historian Josephus also wrote of this period, saying the Syrians "indulged all sorts of the extremist wickedness, and tormented the worthiest of the inhabitants (of Judea) man by man and threatened their city every day with open destruction."[1]

In his *Antiquities of the Jews*, Josephus wrote,

(Antiochus) left the temple bare; and took away the golden candlesticks, and the golden altar [of incense] and table [of shew bread] and the altar [of burnt offering]. He did not abstain from even the veils, which were made of fine linen and scarlet. He also emptied it of its secret treasures; and left nothing at all remaining: and by this means cast the Jews into great lamentation. He also forbade them to offer those daily sacrifices which they used to offer to God, according to the law. And when he had pillaged the whole city, some of the inhabitants he slew, and some he carried captive. . . . He also burnt down the finest buildings, and when he had overthrown the city walls, he built a citadel. . . .

And when the king had built an idol altar upon God's altar he slew swine upon it. . . . He also compelled them to forsake the worship which they paid their own God, and to adore those whom he took to be gods; and made them build temples and raise idol altars in every city and village; and offer swine upon them every day.

> . . . [those who opposed him] were whipped with rods; and their bodies were torn to pieces and were crucified, while they were still alive and breathed. They also strangled those women and their sons whom they had circumcised, as the king had appointed, hanging their sons about their necks as they were upon crosses. And if there were any sacred book, or the law found, it was destroyed; and those with whom they were found miserably perished also.[2]

All this took place between the days of the Old and New Testaments, roughly one hundred sixty years before the birth of Christ and more than three hundred years after the days of Daniel. Yet it all happened exactly as Daniel predicted.

But the story becomes even more interesting. The Syrian assault, which according to Josephus included troops on elephants, precipitated a revolt by a Jewish insurgent group led by the Maccabee family. The word *Maccabee* means "Hammer." Using guerrilla warfare, the Jews miraculously managed to defeat the Syrians. In 164 BC, Jerusalem was recaptured by the Maccabees and the temple reconsecrated. This victory is celebrated by the Jewish people every year by the holy season of Hanukkah.

It took another twenty years to force the Seleucids totally out of the land, but Israel finally became its own independent nation in 142 BC, after more than five hundred years of subjection to the Assyrians, Babylonians, Persians, Greeks, and Syrians—the cast of characters outlined in Daniel's prophecies.

What happened to Antiochus?

Second Maccabees 9 says that when Antiochus heard of the defeat of his forces in Judea, he became furious and ordered his chariot toward Jerusalem to

> turn [it] into a graveyard full of Jews. But he did not know that he was heading straight for God's judgment. In fact, as soon as

he had said these words, the all-seeing Lord, the God of Israel, struck him down with an invisible but fatal blow. He was seized with sharp intestinal pains for which there was no relief. . . . But suddenly he fell flat on the ground and had to be carried off on a stretcher. . . . Even the eyes of this godless man were crawling with worms and he lived in terrible pain and agony. The stink was so bad that his entire army was sickened, and no one was able to come close enough to carry him around. . . . And so, this murderer, who had cursed God, suffered the same terrible agonies he had brought on others, and then died a miserable death in the mountains of a foreign land. (GNT)

The Maccabean account might be overdramatized. Historians believe Antiochus died of epilepsy, madness, or disease. Josephus, writing in the first century, explained that when Antiochus learned his forces had been defeated in Judea,

he was confounded, and by the anxiety he was in fell into a distemper, which lasted a great while, and as his pains increased upon him, so he at length perceived he should die in a little time. So he called his friends to him and told them that his distemper was severe upon him and confessed withal that this calamity was sent upon him for the miseries he had brought upon the Jewish nation while he plundered their temple and condemned their God. And when he had said this, he gave up the ghost.[3]

## The Future Fulfillment of Daniel's Predictions

This is not merely an episode from history. The prophecies in Daniel clearly point to a future replication of this event on a much larger scale. The horrific moment when Antiochus placed the statue of Zeus in the temple is a foreshadowing of the middle of the tribulation when the Antichrist will place his own image—the abomination of desolation—in the temple, triggering the three and a half years of great tribulation. It will be history repeating itself.

Let's go back to Daniel 8 and review what Gabriel told Daniel about his dream of the goat and the ram:

> I am going to tell you what will happen later in the time of wrath, because the vision concerns the appointed time of the end. The two-horned ram that you saw represents the kings of Media and Persia. The shaggy goat is the king of Greece, and the large horn between its eyes is the first king. The four horns that replaced the one that was broken off represent four kingdoms that will emerge from his nation but not have the same power.
>
> In the latter part of their reign, when rebels have become completely wicked, a fierce-looking king, a master of intrigue, will arise. He will become very strong, but not by his own power. He will cause astounding devastation and will succeed in what-ever he does. He will destroy those who are mighty, the holy people. He will cause deceit to prosper, and he will consider himself superior. When they feel secure, he will destroy many and take his stand against the Prince of princes. Yet he will be destroyed, but not by human power.
>
> The vision of the evenings and mornings that has been given to you is true, but seal up the vision, for it concerns the distant future. (vv. 19–26)

This one prediction has a double fulfillment. Its first iteration was in Antiochus IV Epiphanes, but he was only a foreshadowing of the distant future and of the Antichrist, who will be completely wicked, a fierce-looking king, a master of intrigue. The Antichrist will become very strong, but not by his own power. He will be infused with satanic force. When the Jews feel secure following the first half of the tribulation, he will destroy many of them and take his stand against the Prince of princes, the Lord Jesus Christ. Yet he will be destroyed, but not by human power. He will be slain by the spoken word of Christ and the breath of His mouth.

Let's also revisit Daniel 11. Here we have a long description of Antiochus/the Antichrist, which includes verses 36 and 37:

> The king [Antiochus/the Antichrist] will do as he pleases. He will exalt and magnify himself above every god and will say unheard-of things against the God of gods [on nearly every occasion in Scripture when the Antichrist is predicted, he is vocally railing against the Lord, blaspheming Him in vilest language].
>
> He will be successful until the time of wrath is completed, for what has been determined must take place. He will show no regard for the gods of his ancestors or for the one desired by women, nor will he regard any god, but will exalt himself above them all.

This seems to imply the Antichrist will be an atheist, so self-centered he can conceive of no one greater than himself. The suggestion that the Antichrist has "no regard for . . . the one desired by women" is a difficult phrase to translate. Many commentators believe it's an allusion to Christ, because so many generations of Hebrew women dreamed of being His mother.

Verse 38 continues: "Instead of them, he will honor a god of fortresses; a god unknown to his ancestors he will honor with gold and silver, with precious stones and costly gifts."

If the Antichrist has any god at all besides his own ego, it will be military might—a level of political and military power unheralded in history. He will pour unimaginable sums of money into the buildup of his armies, navies, and weaponry. Yet all of it will end for him at Armageddon, when "he will come to his end, and no one will help him" (v. 45).

The passage goes on to say this reign of terror by the Antichrist will be "a time of distress such as has not happened from the beginning of nations until then" (Daniel 12:1). Jesus used this same phrase to describe the great tribulation in Matthew 24:21.

Afterward, the Lord will return and bring the Antichrist to his end. Then the godly will be resurrected and "will shine like the brightness of the heavens, and those who lead many to righteousness, like the stars forever and ever" (Daniel 12:3). In verse 9, we're told these events are not just about a coming Syrian ruler. The words are "rolled up and sealed until the time of the end."

## New Testament Confirmation

Antiochus IV served as a sneak peek of the Antichrist. He terrorized and sought to destroy the nation of Israel, invaded the temple, and set up an abominable image that desolated it. All that occurred one hundred sixty years before New Testament times. But Jesus predicted a future and ultimate fulfillment to Daniel's writings when He said, "When you see standing the holy place the 'abomination that causes desolation,' spoken of through the prophet Daniel— let the reader understand—then let those who are in Judea flee to the mountains. . . . For then there will be great distress, unequalled from the beginning of the world until now—and never to be equaled again" (Matthew 24:15–16, 21).

Jesus wasn't speaking of a past event, but of the future.

The apostle Paul foresaw the return of Christ would be preceded by an Antiochus-type figure: "a man of lawlessness . . . the man doomed to destruction. He will oppose and will exalt himself over everything that is called God or is worshipped, so that he sets himself up in God's temple, proclaiming himself to be God" (2 Thessalonians 2:3–4).

The Antichrist, then, will be an atheist whose only god is himself and his power. His own image is the one he'll set up in the rebuilt Jewish temple. It won't be Zeus. It will be him!

And that's exactly what we read in Revelation as more details emerge. It will be an image possessed with supernatural force, erected by the False Prophet, the third member of the diabolical trinity. Revelation 13 says,

> *It [the False Prophet] ordered them to set up an image in honor of the beast who was wounded by the sword and yet lived [the Antichrist]. The second beast [the False Prophet] was given power to give breath to the image of the first beast, so that the image could speak and cause all who refused to worship the image to be killed.* (vv. 14–15)

I'm amazed at the consistency of the prophetic threads that wind through Scripture!

Those are specific predictions, repeated, confirmed by past fulfillment, and awaiting a future consummation. But don't ask me who the Antichrist will be or if he is alive now. That's beyond my knowledge. We shouldn't look at particular current personalities on the world stage and speculate if they might be the Antichrist. He will come in his appointed time, and he will be so popular and powerful that few will see his diabolical and dark heart, at least at first.

Yet consider one more thing.

I don't think Antiochus IV was the only forerunner of the Antichrist. Starting with Nimrod, we've had a series of powerful, evil rulers who have opposed Christ, who have been anti-God. Many of them have sought to destroy the Jewish people—for example, Pharaoh in Exodus 14, Haman in the book of Esther, and Hitler in more recent times.

The apostle John spoke of the coming Antichrist, but he warned us that the spirit of the antichrist is already in the world now. We must be on our guard and, whatever happens, maintain our eternal allegiance to our Lord Jesus Christ.

I will close this discussion with the clarifying and encouraging words of 1 John 4:3–4: "Every spirit that does not acknowledge

Jesus is not from God. This is the spirit of the antichrist, which you have heard is coming and even now is already in the world. You, dear children, are from God and have overcome them, because the one who is in you is greater than the one who is in the world."

# Gog and Magog

## *A Verse-by-Verse Study of Ezekiel 38–39*

The battle of Armageddon—as famous as it is in popular thinking—is given only a slight description in the book of Revelation. We're told in Revelation 16:16 that the demonic spirits working with the Antichrist "gathered the kings together to a place that in Hebrew is called Armageddon." These armies are slain "with the sword coming out of the mouth of the rider on the horse" (Revelation 19:21), referring to the victorious shout of Christ.

The battle of Armageddon is the war waged against Jerusalem at the very end of the great tribulation. Why didn't John go into more detail? Why didn't he describe the war more fully?

Part of the reason may be this: the prophet Ezekiel devoted two long chapters to just this very battle, and John was writing against the backdrop of the information he knew very well from Ezekiel 38–39. This is the famous battle of Gog and Magog, which, in my opinion, is one and the same with the battle of Armageddon.

Eminent scholar Charles Lee Feinberg wrote of Ezekiel 38–39, "They tell, if interpreted literally, of a coming northern confederacy of nations about the Black and Caspian Seas with Persia and North

Africa, who will invade the promised land after Israel's restoration to it."[1]

That sums up the chapters in one accurate sentence. Furthermore, Feinberg suggests the most reasonable time period for this war is "the end of the tribulation period before Christ is visibly manifested to the world (see Zechariah 14:1–2). The armies of chapters 38 and 39 would appear to be included in the universal confederacies seen in Zechariah 12 and 14."[2]

The best way to study this passage is to work our way through it verse by verse. So let's do that.

Chapter 38 begins,

*The word of the LORD came to me: [2]"Son of man, set your face against Gog, . . .*

After Ezekiel predicted the political return of the Jews to a reestablished nation of Israel in chapters 36–37, the Lord told him to preach a sermon of condemnation against someone called Gog. The meaning of the word *Gog* is uncertain, but apparently it is a title rather than a proper name, something like Leader or King or General. This perplexed the Jews of the Second Temple period.

It's also possible the word *Gog* is derived from the Sumerian term *gug*, meaning "darkness."

The *New American Commentary* suggests Gog may be a cryptogram (a coded or encrypted word) for Babylon. One reason this makes sense is because when Ezekiel condemned the various nations that were oppressing Israel in Ezekiel 25–32, Babylon was strangely missing. We would expect him to begin or end his condemnations of the nations with Babylon, as Jeremiah did. If Gog could be identified with Babylon, that would correspond with other scriptures that indicate the great enemy of God's people from Genesis to Revelation is godless and God-hating Babylon. Gog, then, would be king of Babylon. The commentary says,

Using Gog as a symbol of Babylon would fit the apocalyptic nature of these chapters. If such is the case, Babylon itself is being used to represent the nations of the world aligned against God's people in the end times. . . . Ezekiel was concerned not about the destruction of the sixth century B.C. Babylon but of the Babylon of the last days, whose destruction would be necessary to facilitate the messianic restoration of Israel that he envisioned in 33:1–37:28. . . . If this identification is correct, Gog was a symbol of the forces of the Antichrist foreseen by Ezekiel. If the word Gog is from the Sumerian *gug* (meaning "darkness"), that would be additional support for treating him as a symbol of "the prince of this world" (John 12:31; 14:30), an appropriate designation that fits the character of end-time Babylon. . . .

Ezekiel was most concerned about the final form of the Babylonian Empire, "Mystery Babylon," which he called "Gog." Using subtle cryptic clues, he identified Gog as the future Babylon that would appear in the last days to oppose God and His people. The anti-God kingdom Ezekiel saw is similar to the picture in Revelation 16:13–14 of "Mystery Babylon" gathering all the nations against God and His people.[3]

Ancient rabbinical writers also interpreted Gog in this way, as the final enemy that would oppose Israel and be defeated by the Messiah. Gog, then, may be a code name for Babylon, or, more specifically, the final evil ruler of a world system known as "Mystery Babylon."

Now we'll move on to the rest of Ezekiel 38:2:

> . . . *the chief prince of Meshek and Tubal; prophesy against him* . . .

Gog is further defined as the chief prince or king of Meshek and Tubal. The American Standard Version says, "the prince of Rosh, Meshech, and Tubal."

These are known regions. They were areas within Asia Minor, or modern-day Turkey. When I was growing up, Rosh was thought to be Russia, but that view is no longer tenable. The *New American Commentary* says, "The geographical area would today include parts of Iran, Turkey, and southern provinces of Russia." Meshek and Tubal are the New Testament areas of Phrygia and Cappadocia— central and western Turkey (Acts 16:6; 1 Peter 1:1).[4]

It's also important to understand that to the people of Israel, the north represented the place of greatest threat, both militarily and spiritually. Military invasions usually came down from the north. And north of Israel were lands of darkness, lands dominated by the god Baal and other spiritual forces of darkness.

Moving on to verses 3 and 4:

> . . . ³*and say: 'This is what the Sovereign* LORD *says: I am against you, Gog, chief prince of Meshek and Tubal.* ⁴*I will turn you around, put hooks in your jaws and bring you out with your whole army— your horses, your horsemen fully armed, and a great horde with large and small shields, all of them brandishing their swords.*

This is an announcement of a coming battle, of a great future war. Verses 3 and 4 add another important element. These lands will be dominated by vast military forces. Gog will have a massive military machine to the north and east of Israel.

> ⁵*Persia, Cush and Put will be with them, all with shields and helmets . . .*

Verse 5 lists additional allies that will make up this coalition of nations coming against Israel in the last days. The first is Persia, which, until 1935, was the name of modern Iran. Cush refers to a large section of Africa, nations right across the Red Sea from modern Saudi Arabia—Sudan, Eritrea, and Ethiopia. The land of Put is today's Libya—in North Africa.

> [6] *. . . also Gomer with all its troops, and Beth Togarmah from the far north with all its troops—the many nations with you.*

Feinberg identifies Gomer as "the hordes of the Cimmerians, tribes that settled along the Danube and Rhine and later formed the Germanic people."[5] Beth Togarmah refers to sections of Armenia. These are lands to the north of Israel between the Black Sea and the Caspian Sea. A glance at an atlas shows the territories mentioned here wrap around Israel for thousands of miles to the north, east, and south. Dr. Michael Heiser also points out that some of these locations (Gomer, Beth-Togarmah, Meshek, and Tubal) also "correspond to Javan, which is the Semitic word for Greece, or the Aegean area." That would be to the west of Israel, indicating that Israel would be attacked from the north, east, west, and south—from all directions.[6]

As I indicated, there's nothing in Ezekiel 38 specifically about Russia. Older translations listed *Meshek* as Rosh, which led a lot of prophecy teachers in the days of the Cold War to associate it with Russia. I remember one popular preacher claiming that Meshek was Moscow and Tubal was Tobolsk. But there is strong evidence the territories in Ezekiel reach to the Black Sea, which is north of Turkey and bordering the southern sectors of Russia. This doesn't mean Russia won't be involved in the final war, but the route of advance will be through Turkey. In the same way, there's nothing in this passage about China, but far Asian armies may well march through Persia as part of the invasion force.

> [7]"*'Get ready; be prepared, you and all the hordes gathered about you, and take command of them.* [8]*After many days you will be called to arms. In future years you will invade a land that has recovered from*

*war, whose people were gathered from many nations to the mountains of Israel, which had long been desolate. They had been brought out from the nations, and now all of them live in safety . . .'"*

The phrases *after many days* and *in future years* indicate the apocalyptic times of the last days. Israel will be restored as a political entity in the Middle East, populated by *people . . . gathered from many nations.* They will be living in safety, which implies treaties of peace have given Israel a sense of security. This is the peace covenant of Daniel 9:27. Just when Israel thinks she's safe, Gog will lead the nations to attack her. The only time such an occasion seems plausible is the middle of the seven years, specified in that incredible verse.

*⁹"'You and all your troops and the many nations with you will go up, advancing like a storm; you will be like a cloud covering the land.'"*

Gog and his military forces will overwhelm the land of Israel. The next verses take us inside the mind of Gog and actually reveal his thoughts to us.

*¹⁰"'This is what the Sovereign LORD says: On that day thoughts will come into your mind and you will devise an evil scheme. ¹¹You will say, "I will invade a land of unwalled villages; I will attack a peaceful and unsuspecting people—all of them living without walls and without gates and bars. ¹²I will plunder and loot and turn my hand against the resettled ruins and the people gathered from the nations, rich in livestock and goods, living at the center of the land.'"*

The merchants of the earth will be greedy for the plunder and loot from the nation of Israel.

*¹³Sheba and Dedan and the merchants of Tarshish and all her villages*

224

*will say to you, "Have you come to plunder? Have you gathered your*
*hordes to loot, to carry off silver and gold, to take away livestock and*
*goods and to seize much plunder?"'*

God knew what was in the Antichrist's mind. In Ezekiel, He predicted it millennia in advance. But the Antichrist is not the originator of the movements of history. Almighty God is at the top of the chessboard, arranging things in a way that will bring evil to judgment. The chapter continues:

[14]*"Therefore, son of man, prophesy and say to Gog: 'This is what the Sovereign* LORD *says: In that day, when my people Israel are living in safety, will you not take notice of it?* [15]*You will come from your place in the far north, you and many nations with you, all of them riding on horses, a great horde, a mighty army.* [16]*You will advance against my people Israel like a cloud that covers the land. In days to come, Gog, I will bring you against my land, so that the nations may know me when I am proved holy through you before their eyes.*

God's purpose is to show Himself holy among the nations.

[17]*"'This is what the Sovereign* LORD *says: You are the one I spoke of in former days by my servants the prophets of Israel. At that time they prophesied for years that I would bring you against them.* [18]*This is what will happen in that day: When Gog attacks the land of Israel, my hot anger will be aroused, declares the Sovereign* LORD. [19]*In my zeal and fiery wrath I declare that at that time there shall be a great earthquake in the land of Israel.*

Verse 17 may mean that Gog represents the ultimate evil against which all the prophets have spoken. But some commentators think a better translation would be, "Are you the one all the prophets have spoken about?" In other words, "Are you the Messiah? Are you the greatest in the earth? Are you the climactic figure in history? No, you are not!"

Just before Jesus returns, a global earthquake will crumble the nations of the world. The cities will collapse. I believe this is the same earthquake as described in Revelation 16:18, preceding the return of Christ.

> *²⁰The fish in the sea, the birds in the sky, the beasts of the field, every creature that moves along the ground, and all the people on the face of the earth will tremble at my presence. The mountains will be over-turned, the cliffs will crumble and every wall will fall to the ground.*

All these descriptions are found in the last days of the great tribulation in Revelation 16. When Christ comes again with the divine sword of judgment in His mouth—His powerful word—He will find the armies of the Antichrist in crisis, in confusion, and reeling from the judgments of the earthquake and the bowls of wrath. The battle of Armageddon will be cut short by the return of Jesus Christ.

> *²¹I will summon a sword against Gog on all my mountains, declares the Sovereign LORD. Every man's sword will be against his brother. ²²I will execute judgment on him with plague and bloodshed; I will pour down torrents of rain, hailstones and burning sulfur on him and on his troops and on the many nations with him. ²³And so I will show my greatness and my holiness, and I will make myself known in the sight of many nations. Then they will know that I am the LORD.'*

Now we move on to Ezekiel 39. For emphasis, much of the material in chapter 38 is repeated in chapter 39. In the first description, we're given insights into Gog's thinking. Now the conflict is told from God's perspective, giving us insight into His thinking:

*39 "Son of man, prophesy against Gog and say: 'This is what the Sovereign* LORD *says: I am against you, Gog, chief prince of Meshek and Tubal.* ²*I will turn you around and drag you along. I will bring you from the far north and send you against the mountains of Israel.* ³*Then I will strike your bow from your left hand and make your arrows drop from your right hand.* ⁴*On the mountains of Israel you will fall, you and all your troops and the nations with you. I will give you as food to all kinds of carrion birds and to the wild animals.'"*

This is exactly what we discover in Revelation 19, following the return of Christ and the defeat of the armies of the world. Revelation 19:17–21 says that when Christ returns to confront the armies of the world gathered against Jerusalem, His coming will throw them into consternation and confusion, and the birds of the air will gather to gorge on the bodies of the slain and on the remains of war horses and other animals.

⁵*"'You will fall in the open field, for I have spoken, declares the Sovereign* LORD. ⁶*I will send fire on Magog and on those who live in safety in the coastlands, and they will know that I am the* LORD. ⁷*I will make known my holy name among my people Israel. I will no longer let my holy name be profaned, and the nations will know that I the* LORD *am the Holy One in Israel.* ⁸*It is coming! It will surely take place, declares the Sovereign* LORD. *This is the day I have spoken of.'"*

The Lord will make known His holy name among His people Israel. This corresponds perfectly with the prophecy in Zechariah 12:9–13:1, which says, "On that day I will set out to destroy all the nations that attack Jerusalem. And I will pour out on the house of David and the inhabitants of Jerusalem a spirit of grace and supplication. They will look on me, the one they have pierced. . . . On that day a fountain will be opened to the house of David and the inhabitants of Jerusalem, to cleanse them from sin and impurity."

Beginning with verse 9 of chapter 39, Ezekiel described the aftermath of this battle, which would also correspond with the first months of the reign of Christ. The bodies of the evil armies and the weaponry will take years to clear from the land.

> [9]*"Then those who live in the towns of Israel will go out and use the weapons for fuel and burn them up—the small and large shields, the bows and arrows, the war clubs and spears. For seven years they will use them for fuel.* [10]*They will not need to gather wood from the fields or cut it from the forests, because they will use the weapons for fuel. And they will plunder those who plundered them and loot those who looted them, declares the Sovereign LORD.'"*

What to do with all the bodies? Or with the skeletal remains of those plucked bare by the vultures? A mass burial site will be needed.

> [11]*"On that day I will give Gog a burial place in Israel, in the valley of those who travel east of the Sea. It will block the way of travelers, because Gog and all his hordes will be buried there. So it will be called the Valley of Hamon Gog.'"*

We don't know where this great valley is, but most commentators think Ezekiel is referring to the Dead Sea, so the location could be somewhere east of the Dead Sea, in some remote desert spot within modern-day Jordan. If by "Sea," Ezekiel meant the Mediterranean Sea, the logical place would be the Valley of Armageddon itself, also known as the Jezreel Valley, the Valley of Megiddo, and the Plain of Esdraelon. The phrase *Hamon Gog* means the "Hordes of Gog." According to Feinberg, the estimated number of corpses to be buried in seven months amounts to 360 million.[7]

> [12]*"For seven months the Israelites will be burying them in order to*

*cleanse the land.* <sup>13</sup>*All the people of the land will bury them, and the day I display my glory will be a memorable day for them, declares the Sovereign* LORD. <sup>14</sup>*People will be continually employed in cleansing the land. They will spread out across the land and, along with others, they will bury any bodies that are lying on the ground.'"*

According to the Mosaic law, an unburied corpse was considered unclean. The entire land will be cleared of bodies and skeletons, and cleansed, and it will take seven months.

*"'After the seven months they will carry out a more detailed search.* <sup>15</sup>*As they go through the land, anyone who sees a human bone will leave a marker beside it until the gravediggers bury it in the Valley of Hamon Gog,* <sup>16</sup>*near a town called Hamonah. And so they will cleanse the land.'"*

A town will be established to coordinate the efforts. The word *Hamonah* means "Multitude," referring to the size of the defeated army. Ezekiel cycled back to a picture in the next passage, unwilling to leave the images of the birds of prey feasting on the fallen. This picture is also described in Isaiah 34, Jeremiah 46, Zephaniah 1, and Revelation 19.

<sup>17</sup>*"Son of man, this is what the Sovereign* LORD *says: Call out to every kind of bird and all the wild animals: 'Assemble and come together from all around to the sacrifice I am preparing for you, the great sacrifice on the mountains of Israel. There you will eat flesh and drink blood.* <sup>18</sup>*You will eat the flesh of mighty men and drink the blood of the princes of the earth as if they were rams and lambs, goats and bulls—all of them fattened animals from Bashan.* <sup>19</sup>*At the sacrifice I am preparing for you, you will eat fat till you are glutted and drink blood till you are drunk.* <sup>20</sup>*At my table you will eat your fill of horses and riders, mighty men and soldiers of every kind,' declares the Sovereign* LORD.

The slain armies of Gog will be like a sacrificial offering to the wild birds and beasts.

The next paragraph moves the action forward into the millennial reign of Christ; as the world regroups, the Lord Jesus takes charge in Jerusalem, and His kingdom is established through Israel on earth. Ezekiel explained why Israel faced such an existential threat and why God delivered her.

> [21]*"I will display my glory among the nations, and all the nations will see the punishment I inflict and the hand I lay on them.* [22]*From that day forward the people of Israel will know that I am the* LORD *their God.* [23]*And the nations will know that the people of Israel went into exile for their sin, because they were unfaithful to me. So I hid my face from them and handed them over to their enemies, and they all fell by the sword.* [24]*I dealt with them according to their uncleanness and their offenses, and I hid my face from them.*
>
> [25]*"Therefore this is what the Sovereign* LORD *says: I will now restore the fortunes of Jacob and will have compassion on all the people of Israel, and I will be zealous for my holy name.* [26]*They will forget their shame and all the unfaithfulness they showed toward me when they lived in safety in their land with no one to make them afraid.* [27]*When I have brought them back from the nations and have gathered them from the countries of their enemies, I will be proved holy through them in the sight of many nations.* [28]*Then they will know that I am the* LORD *their God, for though I sent them into exile among the nations, I will gather them to their own land, not leaving any behind.* [29]*I will no longer hide my face from them, for I will pour out my Spirit on the people of Israel, declares the Sovereign* LORD.*"*

According to Revelation 20:7–8, Satan will be released at the end of the thousand-year reign of Christ, and he will try to replicate the battle of Gog and Magog, endeavoring to gather the armies of the world in a final effort to destroy Jerusalem. He'll not have the services of the Antichrist or False Prophet, who will already be in hell. This time, a blast of fire from heaven will devour all opponents, and the devil will be thrown into hell with his cohorts. The millennial reign of Christ, then, will open and close with separate versions of the battle of Gog and Magog. Christ will have a double victory, allowing Him to both begin and end His earthly reign with triumphant judgments against evil and with unquestioned eternal supremacy.

# A Final Word

Have I correctly interpreted every verse of Revelation?

Probably not. But the contents of this consummating book of Scripture are so thrilling to me that I wanted to share them with you as best I could.

Even more, I want to share the Lord Jesus Christ of whom these verses speak. In Revelation, we see Him enthroned in His exalted glory, shining like a billion suns, walking among His churches, loving His people, hating evil, bringing all things under His authority, occupying His matchless throne, and ushering us into everlasting Glory.

The world is going to be swept away, but how wonderful is the future of those who know their Lord!

Remember the final invitation of Revelation—and of the entire Bible:

> The Spirit and the bride say, "Come!" And let the one who hears say, "Come!" Let the one who is thirsty come; and let the one who wishes take the free gift of the water of life. (Revelation 22:17)

Note the threefold invitation: Come! Come! Come!

The Lord your Creator has a gift for you, free and freely offered. Eternal life!

Jesus came to earth—God made flesh—to live righteously, die sacrificially, and rise triumphantly. He bids you come and follow Him. The days ahead may be dark, but He is Light itself. The times to come may harbor tribulation, but He offers Glory. The globe is gripped with hatred, but He is the very embodiment of love.

He loves *you*!.

Life on earth is briefer than brief, but eternity is longer than time. Why not give Him your whole heart, life, soul, future, and destiny?

Take this opportunity to . . . Come! Come! Come!

Let the one who wishes take the free gift of the water of life.

*Dear Lord,*
*I confess my faults, failures, sins, and sorrows. Forgive me of all within me that needs forgiveness, and heal me of all my inner wounds. I believe Jesus died, rose again, and is coming back. I give Him my life, for now and always. May I know Him and make Him known as I eagerly await His glorious return, in Jesus' name, amen!*

# Acknowledgments

So many people to thank!

Sealy and Matt Yates have been my literary agents for years and will be, I hope, for years to come. They paved the way for this project and encouraged me throughout the process.

The team at W Publishing is the best. I can't express how much I enjoy working with my publisher, Damon Reiss. Years ago—decades ago—Kyle Olund guided me through *The Red Sea Rules* project, and it's been so much fun working with him again. Carrie Marrs, senior editor at W, has the patience of Job and the insights of Solomon. Allison Carter knows everyone on earth and can get in touch with them. Debbie Eicholtz and Denise Froehlich created a stunning interior design that makes a complex book like this easy to navigate.

The team at Clearly Media works with me behind the scenes with precision. Joshua Rowe and his team help launch every project and keep it in orbit. Clearly Media's graphic artist, Brandon Riesgo, created the images and diagrams inside these pages.

My assistant and associate, Sherry Anderson, has shown up in the acknowledgments of almost all my books. They would have been impossible without her.

Last but not least, thank you, Luke Tyler. You have a job forever as my intern—if you want it!

# Notes

## Introduction: The Trajectory of Our Times

1. J. Barton Payne, *Encyclopedia of Bible Prophecy* (New York: Harper & Row, 1973), 13. According to Payne, there are 8,352 verses (out of a total of 31,124 in the whole Bible) that are predictive. That is 27 percent. The breakdown: In the Old Testament, there are 6,641 verses out of 23,210 (28.5 percent), and in the New Testament, there are 1,711 verses out of 7,914 (21.5 percent).

## Chapter 2: Next Stop: Patmos

1. Parmy Olsen, "Europe's Most Idyllic Places to Live," *Forbes*, September 3, 2009, http://www.forbes.com/2009/09/03/europe -most-idyllic-places-lifestyle-real-estate.html.
2. See, for example, Paige Patterson, *The New American Commentary: Revelation* (Nashville, TN: Broadman & Holman, 2012), 51.
3. See W. A. Criswell, *Expository Sermons on Revelation: Vol. 1* (Grand Rapids, MI: Zondervan, 1969), 38.
4. Adela Collins, "Patmos," ed. Paul J. Achtemeier, *Harper's Bible Dictionary* (San Francisco, CA: Harper & Row, 1985), 755.
5. "Patmos to Ephesus Distance, Location, Road Map and Direction," DistanceBetween2.com, accessed October 7, 2021, http:// distancebetween2.com/patmos/ephesus.
6. There is an alternative way of looking at this verse. It depends on whether you put a comma or a colon after the word *seen* in verse 19. It could be *Write, therefore, what you have seen:* (1) *What*

*is now* (chapters 1–3) *and* (2) *what will take place later* (chapters 4–22). This is not a big difference in interpretation. While most Greek experts prefer the latter, most English students of the Bible (including me) prefer the former, giving the book of Revelation a threefold division.

## Chapter 3: Christ's Final Messages to the Churches

1. "Casting Light on 'Angel,'" Merriam-Webster, accessed November 7, 2021, https://www.merriam-webster.com/words-at-play/word -history-of-angel.
2. Everett Ferguson, "Angels of the Churches in Revelation 1–3: *Status Quaestionis* and Another Proposal," *Bulletin for Biblical Research* 21, no. 3 (2011): 371–86, https://www.jstor.org/stable/26424375.
3. The assumption that the apostle John lived and wrote from Ephesus goes back to Irenaeus, as noted by Leon Morris in *The New International Commentary on the New Testament: The Gospel According to John* (Grand Rapids, MI: Eerdmans, 1971), 59. See also Colin G. Kruse, *The Letters of John* (Grand Rapids, MI: Eerdmans, 2020), 13–14.

## Chapter 4: The Foreseeable Future

1. I admit my numbering of these events is my own construct. I could have listed forty-nine or fifty-one without changing the order or arrangement of the events. Since fifty is a round number and covers all the contents, I chose that number. By breaking down some of the events in chapters 4 and 5, for example, or in chapters 21–22, I could have added more steps. By combining events, I could have enumerated fewer steps. There's nothing inspired or infallible about my numbering. It's a teaching tool to simplify the material and aid in understanding its flow.

## Events Section 1: The First Half of the Tribulation

1. Some leading pretribulation advocates are David Jeremiah, J. Dwight Pentecost, Tim LaHaye, Craig Blaising, and John MacArthur. Midtribulationists are represented by Harold Ockenga and Norman Harrison. Pre-Wrath tribulationists include Marvin Rosenthal, Alan Kurschner, Alan Hultberg, and Robert Van

Kampen. Post-tribulationism is advocated by William Lane Craig, John Piper, George Ladd, and Douglas Moo.

2. Charles W. Cooper, "A Jasper Stone, Clear as Crystal," https://biblicalstudies.org.uk/pdf/churchman/042-01_047.pdf.

3. See, for example, Mal Couch, *A Bible Handbook to Revelation* (Grand Rapids, MI: Kregel, 2001), 226.

4. I'm surprised how often I'm asked if angels sing. The actual Greek verb simply means "to communicate orally," and it could describe either speaking or singing. I have little doubt angels sing. God has created all His creation to sing, from howling dogs to chirping insects. Think of the songbirds and of the great choirs of human voices. If a voice didn't have tonal qualities, it would be a constant monotone. The idea that God would consign the worship leaders in heaven to a constant monotone doesn't seem plausible. So, yes, I use the word *sing* to describe the angelic hymns in Revelation.

5. Dictionary.com, s.v. "tribulation," accessed November 7, 2021, https://www.dictionary.com/browse/tribulation.

6. *Encyclopaedia Britannica Online*, s.v. "Baal," accessed November 7, 2021, https://www.britannica.com/topic/Baal-ancient-deity.

7. Michael Heiser, *The Unseen Realm* (Bellingham, WA: Lexham Press, 2015), 366.

8. Toby Ord of Oxford University and Angus Mercy of the Centre for Long-Term Resilience wrote, "By our estimates—weighing the different probabilities of events ranging from asteroid impact to nuclear war—the likelihood of the world experiencing an existential catastrophe over the next 100 years is one in six." It bears asking, Would we take a plane if there were a one in six chance of it crashing? Ord goes on to say, "We cannot survive many centuries operating at a level of extreme risk like this. And, as technology accelerates, there is strong reason to believe the risks will only continue to grow. . . . We do not know which extreme risk event will come next. It might be another pandemic. Or it might be something completely different, such as a threat from emerging technology." Toby Ord, "Politicians Need to Pay Attention to Existential Risks," *WIRED*, August 8, 2021, https://www.wired.co.uk/article/existential-risk-catastrophe-future-proof.

9. "Hunger and War," *National Geographic*, January 15, 2020, https://www.nationalgeographic.org/article/hunger-and-war/.

10. Tom Whipple and Oliver Moody, "Stephen Hawking on Humanity (and Jeremy Corbyn)," *The Times*, March 7, 2017, https://www.thetimes.co.uk/article/hawking-on-humanity-and-corbyn-jk88zx0w2?region=global. Mary Bowerman, "Stephen Hawking: Technological Advances 'May Destroy Us All,'" *USA Today*, March 7, 2017, https://www.usatoday.com/story/tech/nation-now/2017/03/07/stephen-hawking-technological-advances-may-destroy-us-all/98841862/.

11. Paige Patterson, *The New American Commentary: Revelation* (Nashville, TN: Broadman & Holman, 2012), 189.

12. One of the most frequently asked questions in Revelation is why the tribe of Dan is omitted from this list. We aren't told and we simply don't know. Levi is listed, and Joseph is given two places by the inclusion of his son. The tribe of Dan does reappear later during the millennium, according to Ezekiel 48:1.

13. "The World Watch List," Open Doors, 2021, accessed November 7, 2021, https://www.opendoorsusa.org/christian-persecution/world-watch-list/.

14. For more information about the persecution taking place in North Korea and the other nations I listed, study The World Watch List, published each year by Open Doors, at OpenDoorsUSA.org/WWL.

15. Frank Gardner, "Iraq's Christians 'Close to Extinction,'" BBC News, May 23, 2019, https://www.bbc.com/news/world-middle-east-48333923.

16. Lindy Lowry, "30 More Christians Arrested in Eritrea—Renounce Your Faith or Go to Jail," Open Doors, June 4, 2019, https://www.opendoorsusa.org/christian-persecution/stories/30-more-christians-arrested-in-eritrea-renounce-your-faith-or-go-to-jail/.

17. Seth Gray, "China Is Exporting Surveillance Technology Used to Track the Christians It Persecutes to Other Countries," *Christianity Daily*, February 13, 2021, https://www.christianitydaily.com/articles/10835/20210213/china-is-exporting-the-surveillance-technology-it-uses-to-track-people-it-persecutes-to-other-countries.htm.

18. "The World Watch List," Open Doors, accessed November 7, 2021.

19. Jessica Udall, "What Does Maranatha Mean in the Bible?,"

Christianity.com, February 12, 2021, https://www.christianity.com
/wiki/christian-terms/what-does-maranatha-mean-in-the-bible.html.

20. Thomas L. Constable, "Notes on Revelation: 2021 Edition,"
Plano Bible Chapel, accessed December 16, 2021, https://www
.planobiblechapel.org/tcon/notes/html/nt/revelation/revelation
.htm#_ftnref471.

21. Eric Mack, "Earth 'Will Be Hit' by an Asteroid, Just Not the Huge
Pair Flying By Now," *Forbes*, September 13, 2019, https://www
.forbes.com/sites/ericmack/2019/09/13/earth-will-be-hit-by-an
-asteroid-just-not-the-huge-pair-flying-by-now/.

22. Stephen Hawking, *Brief Answers to the Big Questions* (New York:
Penguin Random House, 2018), 159.

23. Frederick W. Danker, s.v. "ἀψίνθιον," *A Greek-English Lexicon of
the New Testament and Other Early Christian Literature*, 3rd ed.
(Chicago: University of Chicago Press, 2000), 161.

24. Fraser Cain, "How Long Does It Take Sunlight to Reach the Earth?,"
Phys.org, April 15, 2013, https://phys.org/news/2013-04-sunlight
-earth.html.

25. "What Would Happen If a 'Supervolcano' Eruption Occurred Again
at Yellowstone?," USGS, accessed November 7, 2021, https://www
.usgs.gov/faqs/what-would-happen-if-a-supervolcano-eruption
-occurred-again-yellowstone?qt-news_science_products=0#qt
-news_science_products.

26. 1 Enoch 21:10. To read the entire twentieth chapter of 1 Enoch, see
https://intertextual.bible/text/1-enoch-21.10-1-peter-3.19. Scholar
Grant R. Osborne suggests the word *abyss* "came to be used for the
'pit' or 'prison house' (1 Enoch 18:14) in which fallen angels were
imprisoned." Grant R. Osborne, s.v. "(1) Descending Star-Angel
Opens the Abyss (9:1)," *Revelation*, Baker Exegetical Commentary
on the New Testament (Grand Rapids, MI: Baker Academic, 2002).
A key text on this is 1 Enoch 18:14: "The angel said, 'this place is
the end of heaven and earth: this has become a prison for the stars
and the host of heaven.'" To read the entire eighteenth chapter of 1
Enoch, see https://intertextual.bible/text/1-enoch-18.15-jude-1.13.
See also Kelley Coblentz Bautch, *A Study of the Geography of 1
Enoch 17–19* (Boston, MA: Brill, 2003), 137, 178; and the Institute
for Biblical & Scientific Studies discussion of Genesis 1:2, "The

Deep," https://www.bibleandscience.com/bible/books/genesis
/genesis1_deep.htm.

27. Walter A. Elwell, s.v. "Abyss," *Evangelical Dictionary of Theology*,
https://www.biblestudytools.com/dictionary/abyss/.

28. Bob Yirka, "Why Scorpion Stings Are So Painful," Phys.org, August 3,
2017, https://phys.org/news/2017-08-scorpion-painful.html.

29. Mark Cartwright, "Hanging Gardens of Babylon," *World History
Encyclopedia*, July 27, 2018, https://www.worldhistory.org/Hanging
_Gardens_of_Babylon/.

30. Michael Heiser and Trey Stricklin, "Revelation 9," May 22, 2021,
*Naked Bible Podcast*, https://nakedbiblepodcast.com/wp-content
/uploads/2021/05/NB-377-Transcript.pdf.

31. "About the Temple Institute," Temple Institute, accessed November
7, 2021, https://templeinstitute.org/about-us/.

32. See, for example, Tim LaHaye, *Revelation Unveiled* (Grand Rapids,
MI: Zondervan, 1999), 187.

## Events Section 2: The Midway Point of the Tribulation

1. Here I interpret the stars as symbolic of angels, but in Revelation
6:13, when "the stars in the sky fell to earth," I interpreted them
as literal stars—and the reason for that is context. When the Bible
talks about catastrophic changes in the physical universe, the use of
sun, moon, and stars seems to be literal, which is paralleled in cross
references. Here the context indicates a rebellion in the unseen
realms. In other cross references, angels are described as stars.

2. Harvey Solomon, "When the Greenbrier and Other Appalachian
Resorts Became Prisons for Axis Diplomats," *Smithsonian Magazine*,
February 21, 2020, https://www.smithsonianmag.com/travel/when
-greenbrier-other-appalachian-resorts-became-prisons-for-axis
-diplomats-180974243/. Joshua E. Keating, "So, How Do You Expel
an Ambassador, Anyway?," *FP*, May 29, 2012, https://foreignpolicy
.com/2012/05/29/so-how-do-you-expel-an-ambassador-anyway/.

3. Keating, "So, How Do You Expel an Ambassador, Anyway?"

4. *Encyclopaedia Britannica Online*, s.v. "Antiochus IV Epiphanes,"
accessed November 7, 2021, https://www.britannica.com
/biography/Antiochus-IV-Epiphanes.

5. Jack Wellman, "What Does the Number Six (6) Mean or Represent

in the Bible," Patheos, June 14, 2015, https://www.patheos.com
/blogs/christiancrier/2015/06/14/what-does-the-number-six-6
-mean-or-represent-in-the-bible/.

### Events Section 3: The Last Half of the Tribulation

1. Gwendolyn Leick, *The Babylonians: An Introduction* (London: Routledge, 2003), 68–69.
2. Henry M. Morris, *The Revelation Record* (Wheaton, IL: Tyndale House, 1983), 348–49.
3. Polish peasants revolted during the Kosciuszko Uprising in 1794, and that year Chrystian Piotr Aigner published a field manual entitled *Short Treatise on Pike and Scythes*, describing the use of these tools in warfare. Wikipedia, s.v. "Chrystian Piotr Aigner," accessed December 26, 2021, https://www.wikibook.wiki/wiki/es /Chrystian_Piotr_Aigner.
4. *Encyclopaedia Britannica Online*, s.v. "Gog and Magog," accessed November 7, 2021, https://www.britannica.com/topic/Gog.
5. "Ocean Pollution: 11 Facts You Need to Know," Conservation.org, accessed November 7, 2021, https://www.conservation.org/stories /ocean-pollution-11-facts-you-need-to-know?.
6. General Mark Milley said, "We're witnessing one of the largest shifts in global geo-strategic power the world has ever witnessed," speaking of China's recent military advances. He also said, "Today [China] has capabilities in space and cyber, land, sea, air, undersea, and they are clearly challenging us regionally. . . . So we have a case here of a country that is becoming extraordinarily powerful, that wants to revise the international order to their advantage. That's going to be a real challenge over the coming years." Since 2018, China has been named as the top defense threat to the United States. There are a number of media reports on this, including Ellen Mitchell and Jordan Williams, "China Triggers Growing Fears for US Military," *The Hill*, November 7, 2021, https://thehill.com/policy/defense/580248 -china-triggers-growing-fears-for-us-military; Ross Anderson, "The Panopticon Is Already Here," *The Atlantic*, September 2020, https://www.theatlantic.com/magazine/archive/2020/09/china-ai -surveillance/614197/; and Chris Buckley and Paul Mozur, "How China Uses High-Tech Surveillance to Subdue Minorities," *New York*

*Times*, May 22, 2019, https://www.nytimes.com/2019/05/22/world
/asia/china-surveillance-xinjiang.html.

7. John MacArthur, *The MacArthur Bible Commentary* (Nashville, TN: Thomas Nelson, 2005), 2025.

8. Walter A. Elwell, s.v. "Armageddon," *Evangelical Dictionary of Theology*, https://www.biblestudytools.com/dictionary/armageddon/.

9. Kristin Baird Rattini, "Was This Ancient Egypt's Greatest Military Leader?," *National Geographic*, June 10, 2019, https://www
.nationalgeographic.com/culture/article/thutmose-iii.

10. For example, see Michael Heiser, "The Mount of Assembly," chap. 41 in *The Unseen Realm* (Bellingham, WA: Lexham Press, 2015).

11. "Built to Order: Myanmar's New Capital Isolates and Insulates Junta," June 24, 2008, *New York Times*, https://www.nytimes.com
/2008/06/24/world/asia/24myanmar-sub.html.

12. R. J. Wilson, "This Abandoned City Is 6 Times the Size of NYC, but No One's Heard of It," Urbo, June 1, 2017, https://www.urbo
.com/content/this-abandoned-city-is-6-times-the-size-of-nyc-but
-no-ones-heard-of-it/.

13. "Babylon as Seen in Scripture: An Introduction to Revelation 17–18," Bible.org, accessed November 7, 2021, https://bible.org
/seriespage/23-babylon-seen-scripture-introduction-rev-17-18.

14. Alyssa Roat, "7 Facts You Didn't Know About Nimrod in the Bible," Crosswalk.com, December 15, 2020, https://www.crosswalk.com
/faith/bible-study/facts-about-nimrod-in-the-bible.html.

15. "The tentacles of Nimrod's defiance have proven to retain long and ineradicable consequences. The rites and philosophy of Babylonian worship were secretive and pagan; the society was violent, indulgent, pagan, self-serving, and steeped in idolatry. . . . Over the centuries the Babel influence has taken on countless forms of cultic, occultic, animistic, and satanic forms. . . . From Marduk and Semiramis came the numerous gods and goddesses of the ancient world, many of which were encountered in Scripture. We can trace the spirit of insipient Babylon from the age of Nimrod to the old fertility cults, to ancient Zoroastrianism, through medieval witchcraft, and into modern cultism, New Age monism, and divisive sectarianism of many descriptions." Bernie

L. Calaway, *Prophecy A-Z: The Complete Eschatological Dictionary* (lulu.com, 2012), 440. See also Donald A. Mackenzie, *Mythology of the Babylonian People* (London: Bracken Books, 1996), especially pages 276–77. This book was first published in 1915 as *Myths of Babylonia and Assyria*.

16. Lamia a-Gailani Werr, "Archaeology and Politics in Iraq," in *Critical Approaches to Ancient Near East*, ed. Brian A. Brown and Marian H. Feldman (Boston, MA: de Gruyter, 2014).

17. Bobby Allyn, "UNESCO Adds Ruins of Ancient Babylon to Its List of World Heritage Sites," NPR, July 5, 2019, https://www.npr.org /2019/07/05/738970664/unesco-adds-ruins-of-ancient-babylon-to -its-list-of-world-heritage-sites.

18. Joel Rosenburg, "Islamic Extremists Are Trying To Hasten the Coming of the Mahdi," *National Review*, September 11, 2015, https://www.nationalreview.com/2015/09/radical-islam-iran -isis-apocalyptic-messiah-mahdi/.

19. Here is a list of references to earthquakes and global cataclysms associated with the second coming: Isaiah 2:19, 21; 13:13; 24:18; 29:5–6; Ezekiel 38:17–23; Joel 2:10; Zechariah 14:4–5; Matthew 24:4–8; Hebrews 12:25–29; Revelation 16:18.

## Events Section 4: The Return of Christ

1. Martin Luther, "A Mighty Fortress Is Our God," 1529, trans. Frederick H. Hedge, 1852, https://hymnary.org/text/a_mighty _fortress_is_our_god_a_bulwark.

2. J. Dwight Pentecost, *Things to Come: A Study in Biblical Eschatology* (Grand Rapids, MI: Zondervan, 1980), 476.

3. W. A. Criswell, *Expository Sermons on Revelation* (Grand Rapids, MI: Zondervan, 1962).

4. Revelation 21:16: "He measured the city with the rod and found it to be 12,000 stadia in length, and as wide and high as it is long." The NIV marginal note converts the distance to "about 1,400 miles or about 2,200 kilometers."

5. Elizabeth Howell, "International Space Station: Facts, History & Tracking, Space, October 13, 2021, https://www.space.com/16748 -international-space-station.html.

6. This is simply my speculation. The new earth will be much larger

than the current earth, and John points out there will be no more sea. Yet there is a river mentioned in chapter 22, and in our current world, the Lord loves dotting His creation with water features. So my best assumption is that there will be bodies of water, but not in such large proportions as on the current earth.

7. Alexis C. Madrigal, "Good News, Facebook! The Root Word for 'Paradise' Originally Meant 'Walled Garden,'" *The Atlantic*, July 20, 2012, https://www.theatlantic.com/technology/archive/2012/07 /good-news-facebook-the-root-word-for-paradise-originally-meant -walled-garden/260140/.

8. Charles Q. Choi, "'Superdeep' Diamonds Hint at Depth of Carbon Cycle," *Scientific American*, September 16, 2011, https://www .scientificamerican.com/article/superdeep-diamonds-hint-at -depth-of-carbon-cycle/.

9. Clara Moskowitz, "Super-Earth Planet Likely Made of Diamond," Space, October 11, 2012, https://www.space.com/18011-super -earth-planet-diamond-world.html.

10. Michelle Starr, "Myriad Exoplanets in Our Galaxy Could Be Made of Diamond and Rock," Science Alert, September 14, 2020, https:// www.sciencealert.com/there-could-be-a-whole-bunch-of-exoplanets -out-there-made-out-of-rock-and-diamond. See also Emma Yasinski, "Outer Space Is a Treasure Chest of Gemstones," *Discover Magazine*, February 4, 2021, https://www.discovermagazine.com/the-sciences /outer-space-is-a-treasure-chest-of-gemstones.

11. Randy Alcorn, *Heaven* (Wheaton, IL: Tyndale House, 2004), 241.

12. *Shekinah* is an English transliteration of a Hebrew word meaning "dwelling." In rabbinic literature it came to refer to the settlings or dwelling of God among His people. See *Dictionary of Comparative Religion*, ed. S. G. F. Brandon (New York: Scribner's Sons, 1970), 573. According to H. L. Drumwright Jr., *shekinah* is a non-biblical term that appeared in the Targums and in the Talmud to describe the glorious presence of God. H. L. Drumwright Jr., *Zondervan Pictorial Encyclopedia of the Bible*, vol. 5, ed. Merrill C. Tenney (Grand Rapids, MI: Zondervan, 1975).

### Appendix 5: Antiochus IV Epiphanes

1. Flavius Josephus, *The Jewish War*, vol. 1, chap. 1, sect. 2.

2. Flavius Josephus, *Antiquities of the Jews*, vol. 7, chap. 5, sect. 4.

3. *Antiquities of the Jews*, vol. 7, chap. 9, sect. 1.

## Appendix 6: Gog and Magog

1. Charles Lee Feinberg, *The Prophecy of Ezekiel* (Eugene, OR: Wipf and Stock, 2003), 218.

2. Feinberg, 218.

3. L. E. Cooper, *The New American Commentary: Ezekiel* (Nashville, TN: Broadman & Holman, 1994), 332.

4. Feinberg, *Prophecy of Ezekiel*, 220.

5. Feinberg, 221.

6. Michael Heiser and Trey Stricklin, "Ezekiel 38–39, Part 2," April 8, 2017, *Naked Bible Podcast*, https://nakedbiblepodcast.com/wp -content/uploads/2017/04/NB-153-Transcript.pdf.

7. Feinberg, *Prophecy of Ezekiel*, 219, 227. This is explained by these calculations. If a million men are occupied for one hundred eighty days, and if each person buried two bodies a day, the total of the dead would be 360 million.

# About the Author

Robert J. Morgan is a writer and speaker who serves as the teaching pastor at The Donelson Fellowship in Nashville. He is the author of *The Red Sea Rules, The Strength You Need, Reclaiming the Lost Art of Biblical Meditation, Then Sings My Soul,* and many other titles, with more than 4.5 million copies in circulation. He is available to speak at conferences and conventions. Contact him at www.robertjmorgan.com.